W9-AAS-940

365 Days
of
Wisdom

Copyright © 2011 by Dr. Yomi Garnett
All rights reserved.

ISBN: 145647586X
EAN-13: 9781456475864
LCCN: 2010919242

365 Days of Wisdom

A Daily Companion for the Soul in Search of Enlightenment

Dr. Yomi Garnett

A Letter to You

Dear Friend,

In writing this book, I have been motivated by a desire to create a handbook of genuine utility, one consisting of positive and uplifting thoughts that will inspire anyone in need of guidance. This is a book of simple truths from many different philosophies and disciplines, backed by relevant scriptures.

Now, because success and happiness are almost always dependent on certain kinds of thoughts that habitually traverse our minds, it becomes highly imperative that we condition our mind and expose our psyche to the right kind of mental activity. Marcus Aurelius, emperor of Rome 2,000 years ago, was considered one of the wisest men of all time. He said, "Our life is what our thoughts make of it."

Permit me to draw a corollary from our common-place electronic appliance, the air conditioner. Just as the air conditioner will make the air crisply cool and healthy, that is how this constellation of wisdom thoughts and nuggets of insight will make your mind powerful and alert enough to change your subconscious thinking to the creative type of thinking that will lead to the success and happiness that you so richly deserve as a child of God.

Backing each day's thought with the appropriate scripture was a deliberate and carefully thought-out concept that was based on what the Bible itself stated clearly in this verse about what its contents will do;

"If ye abide in me, and my words abide in you, ye shall ask what ye will, and it shall be done unto you."

John 15:7 (KJV)

Throughout the book, I have deliberately employed, in the main, an upbeat, conversational tone. This was predicated on a perceived need to make the entire encounter one that is as interactive as I could conceivably make it.

What I humbly present to you is the result of years of laborious and intensive research into the well trodden path of self-development and spiritual rejuvenation, resulting ultimately in the crystallization of the personal, profound insights, and the harsh lessons that I learnt during my own years of the locust.

Be that as it may, I have not been entirely able to resist the temptation to quote directly from the works of a host of wise men and women who all happen to be my own mentors and role models. In all such cases, I have duly acknowledged the authorship of such quotes.

The entries in the book run the whole gamut of life's experiences, touching on subjects as diverse as spiritual and secular leadership, commerce and industry, human psychology, wealth and prosperity, the human emotions, and a whole host of subjects too numerous to detail here.

The book you hold in your hands is a devotional of sorts, and yet, strictly speaking, it is not one. Rather, I would elect to call it a companion. It was designed to possess great utilitarian value as a handbook of action techniques for wise and correct living. To this end, therefore, may I suggest that the book can be useful to you in three ways:

1. You can read it wholesale as you would any other book.

2. You can, at the start of each day, read the day's entry and meditate on it all day long.

3. If you have a problem, or if you face a stressful situation, you can pray about it, meditate on it, and then randomly open the book. The page you randomly open to, by His special grace, will offer you sufficient insight and direction with which to confront your problem. This is called guidance, and its real source is predicated on a subconscious need, backed by spiritual energy, to seek appropriate answers to life's puzzles and dilemmas. Essentially, this is what is meant by an action technique.

This book is unique in another respect. The layout of each page is such that you can put down your own thoughts and observations, should you choose to do so. This, of course, permits you the rare luxury of turning the entire book into a personalized workbook of sorts.

In cases, however, where there is insufficient page space, you can make your notes on the last pages of the book.

On a rather personal note, this spiritual and literary adventure has profoundly humbled me by leaving me in even greater reverence for the awesome completeness of the Bible.

While wishing you a wonderful year filled with God's blessings, goodness and mercies,

I remain,

Yours affectionately,

Dr. Yomi Garnett
Abuja and Kaduna
Nigeria
May 2009

"But the wisdom that comes from heaven is first of all pure; then peace loving, considerate, submissive, full of mercy and good fruit, impartial and sincere."

James 3:17 (NIV)

January 1

"You are long overdue for your flight, and as God Himself has arranged for you to be on this flight, you will not miss it. And so, in welcoming you aboard this supernatural flight on the wings of the eagle, I urge you not to disregard the grace of God, but to maximize the opportunities around you."

Bishop David O. Oyedepo

"And to the woman were given two wings of a great eagle, that she might fly into the wilderness, into her place, where she is nourished for a time, and times, and half a time, from the face of the serpent."

Revelations 12:14 (NIV)

January 2

In many respects, life is a game. And since you are alive, it means that for you, the game of life is already scheduled. You simply have to play in it. You might as well play to win. So, affirm to yourself today:

"I have reached the point now that I know I'm a winner, and I'll be a winner as long as I'm in this game called life."

"Know ye not that they which run in a race run all, but one receiveth the prize? So run, that ye may obtain."

1 Corinthians 9:24 (KJV)

January 3

It is so much easier to remain in the same comfortable spot, is it not? But consider this. When you want something you have never had, is it not an incontrovertible fact that you will have to do something you have never done before? Today, resolve to move out of your comfort zone.

"Now the Lord had said unto Abram, Get thee out of thy country, and from thy kindred, and from thy father's house, unto a land that I will shew thee."

Genesis 12:1 (KJV)

January 4

"Give us this day our daily bread." This is one of the most consistent prayers in the life of a Christian. But quite often, as we eat this daily bread and become well fed, we tend to forget from whom it all has come. Give credit to whom credit is due.

_____
_____
_____
_____
_____
_____
_____
_____
_____
_____
_____

"But thou shalt remember the Lord thy God: for it is he that giveth thee power to get wealth, that he may establish his covenant which he sware unto thy fathers, as it is this day."

Deuteronomy 8:18 (KJV)

January 5

Divine direction is a function of divine wisdom, and divine wisdom is a function of divine instruction. Put quite simply, the natural sequence is this: Divine instruction leads to divine wisdom, which leads to divine direction.

"Hear instruction, and be wise, and refuse it not."

Proverbs 8:33 (KJV)

January 6

Prosperity does not create excellence. Rather, the reverse is what holds true. Excellence creates prosperity. Therefore, from today, start the process of discovering your own personal excellence; your own best path to fulfillment. Then, every day, walk that path to your prosperity.

_____

_____

_____

_____

_____

_____

_____

_____

_____

_____

_____

"As every man hath received the gift, even so minister the same one to another, as good stewards of the manifold grace of God."

1 Peter 4:10 (KJV)

January 7

One of the most unfortunate, and no less tragic, facts of our existence is that we tend to approach life backwards. It seems we are more inclined to be in reverse gear all the time, giving the most attention to the least important and the least attention to the most important.

_____

_____

_____

_____

_____

_____

_____

_____

_____

_____

_____

"Receive my instruction, and not silver; and knowledge rather than choice gold. For wisdom is better than rubies; and all the things that may be desired are not to be compared to it."

Proverbs 8:10–11 (KJV)

January 8

Those who attain true success are those who derive joy and happiness as they invest their time and energy in worthwhile pursuits. This is hardly surprising, for true success is not merely a destination, but a journey. If a journey is truly worthwhile, should it not also be pleasurable?

_____

_____

_____

_____

_____

_____

_____

_____

_____

_____

_____

"I know that there is no good in them, but for a man to rejoice, and to do good in his life. And also that every man should eat and drink, and enjoy the good of all his labour, it is the gift of God."

Ecclesiastes 3:12–13 (KJV)

January 9

One man says his goal is to own a Peugeot 406 car by the end of the year. Another says he desires to own a Peugeot 406 car by the end of the year. On the surface, they both seem to be saying the same thing. But they are not. You see, goals and desires differ. You can have a desire, and not act on it, since a desire is a mere wish and can even be a passing fancy. But you cannot have a goal and not act on it.

_____

_____

_____

_____

_____

_____

_____

_____

_____

_____

"He who works his land will have abundant food, but he who chases fantasies lacks judgment."

Proverbs 12:11 (KJV)

January 10

You can only hit that at which you aim. So, you are better off aiming very high. Strive for lofty goals. Yes, indeed, dream big dreams. You see, the problem with weak dreams is that they can only inspire weak efforts.

_____

_____

_____

_____

_____

_____

_____

_____

_____

_____

_____

"Now unto him that is able to do exceedingly abundantly above all that we ask or think, according to the power that worketh in us. Unto him be glory in the church by Christ Jesus throughout all ages, world without end, Amen."

Ephesians 3:20–21 (KJV)

January 11

No man is wise enough by himself.

"*For the Lord giveth wisdom; out of his mouth cometh knowledge and understanding.*"

Proverbs 2:6 (KJV)

January 12

You don't have to be a geologist to know that some stones are smooth to the touch, while others are rough. It is also common knowledge that a stone cannot be smooth and polished without sustained friction. It is the same with you. You cannot be perfected without trials.

"It is good for me that I have been afflicted; that I might learn thy statutes."

Psalm 119:71 (KJV)

January 13

"Sow an act; reap a habit,
Sow a habit; reap a character,
Sow a character; reap a destiny."

Charles Reade (1814–1884)
British Novelist

_____

_____

_____

_____

_____

_____

_____

_____

_____

"See then that ye walk circumspectly, not as fools, but as wise.
Redeeming the time, because the days are evil."

Ephesians 15:15–16 (KJV)

January 14

Prepare for your success in little ways, and you will see the result in big ways. As you plan for what is ahead, first check what is near at hand. As you strive for the great, do be careful about the small.

_____

_____

_____

_____

_____

_____

_____

_____

_____

_____

_____

_____

_____

"Go to the ant, thou sluggard; consider her ways, and be wise. Which having no guide, overseer, or ruler, provideth her meat in the summer, and gathereth her food in the harvest."

Proverbs 6:6–8 (KJV)

January 15

It is imperative that we cultivate an attitude of gratitude that is unique in its consistency. This will allow us to express honest appreciation to all who help us in one way or the other. However, we must never fake this appreciation. But if we feel it, we must express it. The expression of gratitude would seem to be a powerful force that generates even more of what we have already received.

"For who maketh thee to differ from another? And what hast thou that thou didst not receive? Now if thou didst receive it, why dost thou glory as if thou hadst not received it?"

1 Corinthians 4:7 (KJV)

January 16

The chef had just recommended that I order the restaurant's mixed grill. He said it was very good. When the dish arrived, it reminded me of life. Life is a mixed grill, isn't it? Every day, we experience many successes, and many failures. However, victory lies in perseverance. If we consistently correct our course, we can repeatedly reposition ourselves as the inheritors of God's abundance. Herein lies the mystery of prosperity.

"Blessed is the man who perseveres under trial, because when he has stood the test, he will receive the crown of life that God has promised to those who love him."

James 1:12 (NIV)

January 17

A friend of mine was once special assistant to a minister of state. This conversation took place between them.

Special Assistant: *"Sir, you hardly ever get disturbed about what people say about you. Why is this so?"*

Minister of State: *"There is an amusing irony in this tendency for people to say unkind things about others. Point your index finger at me, please. Now, what are your three other fingers doing?"*

Special Assistant: *"They are pointing back at me, sir!"*

Minister of State: *"You see! I win three to one. Someone points one finger at me, but three accusing fingers point back at him!"*

"Therefore thou art inexcusable, O man, whosoever thou art that judgest: for wherein thou judgest another, thou condemnest thyself, for thou that judgest doest the same things."

Romans 2:1 (KJV)

January 18

There are few guarantees in life; but a lot of opportunities if you are willing to step out boldly. Yes, indeed, unlimited opportunities surround you. It's just that they are disguised as seemingly insurmountable obstacles.

_____

_____

_____

_____

_____

_____

_____

_____

_____

_____

_____

_____

"For unto every one that hath shall be given, and he shall have abundance: but from him that hath not shall be taken away even that which he hath."

Matthew 25:29 (KJV)

January 19

"The greater the difficulty;
the greater the glory"

Cicero (106–43 BC)
Roman Orator and Statesman

_____

_____

_____

_____

_____

_____

_____

_____

_____

_____

_____

"And the women answered one another as they played, and said;
Saul hath slain his thousands, and David his ten thousands."

1 Samuel 18:7 (KJV)

January 20

Be patient with the faults of others. They have to be patient with yours. This seemingly simple statement may be clear enough indication that patience, in itself, may be a much more spiritual attribute than we ordinarily realize. Pray, today, that God may grant you the grace to be patient with others.

"Judge not, and ye shall not be judged: condemn not, and ye shall not be condemned: forgive, and ye shall be forgiven."

Luke 6:37 (KJV)

January 21

If not now, then when? If not you, then who? Act now!

Rabbi Hillel

Do not spend so much time preparing for the trip that you end up not taking it at all. Over preparation can be as bad as under preparation. Make that move!

"How long wilt thou sleep, O sluggard? When wilt thou arise out of thy sleep? Yet a little sleep, a little slumber, a little folding of the hands to sleep. So shall thy poverty come as one that travelleth, and thy want as an armed man."

Proverbs 6:6–9 (KJV)

January 22

A claim by anyone of a lifetime of completely uninterrupted success can, at best, only be described as dubious, as no one experiences one success after another without some dose of defeat and failure along the way. The ability to overcome the times of agony is what separates winners from losers.

_____
_____
_____
_____
_____
_____
_____
_____
_____
_____
_____
_____

"After Job had prayed for his friends, the Lord made him prosperous again and gave him twice as much as he had before."

Job 42:10 (KJV)

January 23

It is aptly said that there are two kinds of people: Those who watch things happen and those who make things happen. It is time for you to seize the day! You see an opportunity, take it! You have an idea, speak up! Remember, nothing ventured, nothing gained.

_____

_____

_____

_____

_____

_____

_____

_____

_____

_____

_____

"And it came to pass in the four hundred and eightieth year after the children of Israel were come out of the land of Egypt, in the fourth year of Solomon's reign over Israel, in the month of Zif, which is the second month, that he began to build the house of the Lord."

1 Kings 6:1 (KJV)

January 24

There is no shame in making mistakes or in falling, since every experience you have is meant to teach you something. But each time you fall, you have to get up again, dust yourself, and start all over again, even if you hear mocking laughter all around you. With each failure, your character becomes stronger and your soul more durable. However, there is one terrible and avoidable failure. It is the failure to learn from your failure.

_____

_____

_____

_____

_____

_____

_____

_____

_____

_____

"As a dog returneth to his vomit, so a fool returneth to his folly."

Proverbs 26:11 (KJV)

January 25

"Those who are certain of the outcome can afford to wait, and without anxiety."

Anonymous Greek Writing

_____

_____

_____

_____

_____

_____

_____

_____

_____

_____

_____

"He hath made everything beautiful in his time; also he hath set the world in their heart, so that no man can find out the work that God maketh from the beginning to the end."

Ecclesiastes 3:11 (KJV)

January 26

One of man's greatest failings is his inability to sit all alone, by himself, to engage in the deep inner activities of contemplation and meditation. Today, commit some time to sit and think. Meditate. This will give you access to the flow of divine wisdom and insight.

_____

_____

_____

_____

_____

_____

_____

_____

_____

_____

_____

_____

"I have more understanding than all my teachers: for thy testimonies are my meditations."

Psalm 119:99 (KJV)

January 27

The person who refuses to hear criticism has no chance to learn from it. Always be ready to see your error and admit it. Resolve to make correction your faithful friend and a necessary means to improvement. To be truly wise, you must remember that at times, you too have played the fool.

_____

_____

_____

_____

_____

_____

_____

_____

_____

_____

"A fool despiseth his father's instruction: but he that regardeth reproof is prudent."

Proverbs 15:5 (KJV)

January 28

Our fundamental nature is basically an acquisitive one, and it is only natural that we seek the material bounties of our world—good homes, cars, clothes, etc. Properly acquired, these are physical manifestations of God's blessings, making them spiritually legitimate. However, how much we possess is not quite as important as our attitude towards these possessions. After all, discontentment makes the rich man poor, while contentment makes the poor man rich. Whatever your status, be content with what you have, neither coveting more nor resenting those who have more than you.

_____
_____
_____
_____
_____
_____
_____

"For we brought nothing into this world, and it is certain we can carry nothing out. And having food and raiment let us be therewith content."

1 Timothy 6:7–8 (KJV)

January 29

Viewed from a spiritual perspective, fear and faith can be said to be opposites. It is also quite true that what each of them brings to our lives are also opposites. Fear can lead to failure. Faith will lead to conquest.

_____

_____

_____

_____

_____

_____

_____

_____

_____

_____

_____

"For God hath not given us the spirit of fear; but of power, and of love, and of a sound mind."

2 Timothy 1:7 (KJV)

January 30

The soul that has no real aim loses itself. This is because if it is well with your soul, you have everything that matters. If, however, it is not well with your soul, then nothing else matters.

_____
_____
_____
_____
_____
_____
_____
_____
_____
_____
_____
_____
_____

"For what is a man profited, if he shall gain the whole world, and lose his own soul? Or what shall a man give in exchange for his soul?"

Matthew 16:26 (KJV)

January 31

Praising yourself to yourself can build self-confidence and be a morale booster. On the other hand, praising yourself to others can breed resentment.

_____

_____

_____

_____

_____

_____

_____

_____

_____

_____

_____

_____

"A prudent man keeps his knowledge to himself, but the heart of fools blurts out folly."

Proverbs 12:23 (KJV)

February 1

Life will give us exactly what we expect from it. No more, no less. Unfortunately, we tend to labor under the grand illusion that life is more inclined to shortchange us while in actual fact, it is generally prepared to deliver to us much more than we realize. With a confident belief in the perfect outcome of every situation, start today to ask, to seek, and to knock.

_____

_____

_____

_____

_____

_____

_____

_____

_____

_____

"Ask, and it shall be given you; seek and ye shall find; knock and it shall be opened unto you."

Matthew 7:7 (KJV)

February 2

"I have often wondered how every man loves himself more than all the rest of men, yet sets less value on his own opinion of himself than on the opinion of others."

Marcus Aurelius (121–180)
Roman Emperor

Many of us are shackled down by what others think of us. Refuse to be burdened by what others think of you, and act only in accordance with divine purpose. To maintain control of your life, you must extricate yourself from the confines of public opinion. Remain faithful to your plan. Keep your life in your own hands.

_____

_____

_____

_____

_____

"Then Peter and the other apostles answered and said; we ought to obey God rather than men."

Acts 5:29 (KJV)

February 3

Today, I invite you to engage in a most unusual exercise. Get a pen and paper. List out one hundred things you would like to accomplish in your lifetime.

"I can do all things through Christ which strengtheneth me."

Philippians 4:13 (KJV)

February 4

Observe yourself, in as detached a manner as possible, when next you are engaged in an animated discussion, possibly a mild argument, with another person. Can you notice how you can hardly wait for him to stop talking before you interject your own words? And that, in fact, you are hardly listening to him? This habit of poor communication is common to most of us. To start to become a better listener, repeat to yourself for the rest of today: "I have two ears and one mouth so that I should listen more and talk less."

"So they sat down with him upon the ground seven days and seven nights, and none spake a word unto him; for they saw that his grief was very great."

Job 2:13 (KJV)

February 5

Do all the good you can, by all the means you can, in all the ways you can, in every place you can, at all the times you can, to everyone you can, as long as you ever can. Count that day lost in which you have not done something good for another person.

_____

_____

_____

_____

_____

_____

_____

_____

_____

_____

_____

_____

"As we have therefore opportunity, let us do good unto all men, especially unto them who are of the household of faith."

Galatians 6:10 (KJV)

February 6

A man was once asked why he always talked to himself. He replied: "I do this for two reasons: first, I like to hear a smart man talk, and second, I like to talk to a smart man." Avoid boasting. If you notice anything in you that puffs you with pride, look very closely and you will find more than enough to make you humble.

_____

_____

_____

_____

_____

_____

_____

_____

_____

_____

_____

_____

"Do not think of yourself more highly than you ought, but rather think of yourself with sober judgement."

Romans 12:3 (KJV)

February 7

Generally, we tend to be uncomfortable with silence. Yet, there is no law against silence. A pregnant silence beats an empty noise any day. Refuse to engage in foolish talk. Engaging in foolish talk is one sure way of depleting your spiritual energy.

"If only you would be altogether silent! For you that would be wisdom."

Job 13:5 (KJV)

February 8

"What we commonly call luck can actually be ascribed to the act of laboring under correct light or knowledge."

Bishop David O. Oyedepo

_____
_____
_____
_____
_____
_____
_____
_____
_____
_____
_____
_____

"When his candle shined upon my head, and when by his light I walked through darkness."

Job 29:3 (KJV)

February 9

"When God gets ready to bless you, He just does. He does it because He can. He does it because it pleases Him to do so. He does it because it fits into some greater purpose."

Bishop T.D. Jakes

When God decides to take you on His divine ride, you don't have to stand by the roadside. He will pick you up at whatever your location happens to be at that precise moment.

_____

_____

_____

_____

_____

"The Lord bless thee, and keep thee:
The Lord make His face shine upon thee,
And be gracious unto thee:
The Lord lift up His countenance upon thee,
And give thee peace."

Numbers 6:24-26 (KJV)

February 10

The times were lean for the thirty-year-old school. Most buildings were in a state of disrepair and there was a three-month backlog of staff salaries. A stranger, who later turned out to be an alumnus, visited the school one day and found a man working on the engine of the school bus.

"Good day, sir. Where can I find the principal?" he asked.

"He should be in his office in about an hour," came the reply.

An hour later, the visitor met the principal in his office and recognized him as the man who was working on the school bus earlier on.

Later that week, the school received a letter and a check for five million naira! The principal's spirit of humble service had made a positive impression.

"For whosoever exalteth himself shall be abased; and he that humbleth himself shall be exalted."

Luke 14:11 (KJV)

February 11

"If you ever think you are too small to be effective, then you have never been in bed with a mosquito."

Anita Roddick

You are not small. On the contrary, you are quite big. The big child of a big God!

_____

_____

_____

_____

_____

_____

_____

_____

_____

_____

"So God created man in his own image."

Genesis 1:27 (NIV)

February 12

In the world of commerce and industry, a big issue is usually made of what people are worth. The higher your net worth, the greater the respect you attract. Ultimately however, our value is determined not by what we have, but by what we do with what we have.

"One man gives freely, yet gains even more; another withholds unduly, but comes to poverty."

Proverbs 11:24 (KJV)

February 13

I once witnessed a target practice at a police shooting range. The similarity to our life experience struck me immediately. The goals we set are actually targets, and in aiming to achieve these goals, we are merely shooting at the targets. So from today, start setting targets; then start shooting at them. You need the target practice. What is more, God's subscription to your target practice is total.

_____

"Open the east window, he said, and he opened it. Shoot. Elisha said, and he shot. The Lord's arrow of victory."

2 Kings 13:17 (NIV)

February 14

Today is Valentine's Day.
Say it with a card. That is good.
Say it with flowers. That is also good.
Say it with a gift. That is good, too.
But, say it in words. That is best.
A word of love can make a world of difference.

_____
_____
_____
_____
_____
_____
_____
_____
_____

"My lover spoke and said to me,
    'Arise, my darling, my beautiful one,
    And come with me.'"

Song of Solomon 2:10 (NIV)

February 15

Trafalgar Square is one of London's more popular tourist sites. It is known for the large number of pigeons that reside there. Worries are very much like these birds. You can't prevent them from flying around your head, but you can keep them from building a nest in your hair. Eliminate worry from your life.

_____

_____

_____

_____

_____

_____

_____

_____

_____

_____

_____

_____

"Who of you by worrying can add a single hour to his life? Since you cannot do this very thing, Why do you worry about the rest?"

Luke 12:25–26 (NIV)

February 16

After attaining a goal, take the afternoon off. But don't take the year off. Today's excellence can easily turn into tomorrow's failure. You see, past successes do not guarantee future victories. So, as you attain your goals, set new ones. You are more likely to enjoy success if you also enjoy seeking it passionately.

_____

_____

_____

_____

_____

_____

_____

_____

_____

_____

_____

_____

"So, if you think you are standing firm, be careful that you don't fall!"

1 Corinthians 10:12 (NIV)

February 17

Today, resolve firmly to communicate your confidence to others. For after all, the source of this confidence is the Divine. Speak with this confidence. Dress for success. Step out gracefully, with impeccable poise and control.

"If God be for us, who can be against us?"

Romans 8:31 (KJV)

February 18

Historical scholars will tell you that the history of mankind is the history of failure and of achievement. They will however quickly add that the history of mankind is also the history of persistence and of conquest.

"To everything there is a season, and a time to every purpose under the heaven."

Ecclesiastes 3:1 (KJV)

February 19

Most people don't plan to fail. They just fail to plan. From today, start to plan your work. Then work the plan.

P	-	*Prepare carefully*
L	-	*Launch out boldly*
A	-	*Adjust as you go*
N	-	*Network with others*

"But the noble man makes noble plans, and by noble deeds he stands."

Isaiah 32:8 (NIV)

February 20

In some cultures, water is seen as a symbol of humility and service. This is because water nurtures and sustains all living things and yet seeks nothing for itself, always flowing to the lowest spot.

Be like water. Be humble. Nurture yourself and others. Remain at the back, where you are free to come and go as you please, unnoticed.

_____

_____

_____

_____

_____

_____

_____

_____

_____

_____

"But he that is greatest among you shall be your servant: And whosoever shall exalt himself shall be abased; and he that shall humble himself shall be exalted."

Matthew 23:11–12 (KJV)

February 21

"It is not enough to have a good mind. The main thing is to use it well."

Rene Descartes (1596–1650)
French Philosopher

"Let this mind be in you which was also in Christ Jesus."

2:5 (KJV)

February 22

The quest for success in life is almost always a journey of effort, frustration, and ultimately, joy. It is also a journey of heart, mind, and body. It is an adventure of challenge, which if faithfully and courageously confronted, will result in triumph.

_____

_____

_____

_____

_____

_____

_____

_____

_____

_____

_____

_____

_____

"Weeping may endure for a night, but joy cometh in the morning."

Psalm 30:5 (KJV)

February 23

The big difference between success and failure is not talent. It is persistence.

_____

_____

_____

_____

_____

_____

_____

_____

_____

_____

_____

"But that on the good ground are they, which in an honest and good heart, having heard the word, keep it and bring forth fruit with patience."

Luke 8:15 (KJV)

February 24

In 1982, I was in my second year in medical school. The late Archbishop Benson Idahosa was invited to lecture my class on the topic "Community Medicine and Religion." It was a most illuminating lecture. His parting words, captured in my lecture notes, were these: "Make prayer an integral and constant part of your daily life. Commit to setting aside regular times for prayer each day. The most powerful position on earth is the kneeling position."

_____

_____

_____

_____

_____

_____

_____

_____

_____

_____

_____

"Pray without ceasing."

1 Thessalonians 5:17 (KJV)

February 25

Pray, not for a lighter load, but for a stronger back. For it is not that you will not be tempted, nor that you will not experience the travails of life. Rather, it is that you will not be overcome.

"There hath no temptation taken you but such as is common to man; but God is faithful, who will not suffer you to be tempted above that ye are able, but will with the temptation also make a way to escape, that ye may be able to bear it."

1 Corinthians 10:13 (KJV)

February 26

"Whatever is supposed to come to your life will be there when you have developed the capacity to receive it."

Dr. Wayne Dyer

_____

_____

_____

_____

_____

_____

_____

_____

_____

_____

_____

"But the one who received the seed that fell on good soil is the man who hears the word and understands it. He produces a crop, yielding a hundred, sixty or thirty times what was sown."

Matthew 13:23 (KJV)

February 27

We, each, have a light burning within us. You have to nourish that light and let it shine for all to see. You will do this by proving the nobility of your love for others, proving the sincerity of your innermost aspirations and desires, proving the greatness of your faith in your mission, and then finally, recognizing that you are greater than failure. And even of success.

_____

_____

_____

_____

_____

_____

"You are the light of the world. A city on a hill cannot be hidden. Neither do people light a lamp and put it under a bowl. Instead, they put it on its stand, and it gives light to everyone in the house. In the same way, let your light shine before men, that they may see your good deeds and praise your father in heaven."

Matthew 5:14–16 (NIV)

February 28

When you do that which you love and you do it skillfully, you will come out with a masterpiece!

_____

_____

_____

_____

_____

_____

_____

_____

_____

_____

_____

_____

_____

_____

"Do you see a man skilled in his work? He will serve before kings, he will not serve before obscure men."

Proverbs 22:29 (NIV)

March 1

I have thought long and hard. I have pondered over all the twists and all the turns in our quest for knowledge and wisdom. I have also considered all our possible motivations for embarking on this arduous journey. Lastly, I have contemplated all the possible returns on investment in physical, emotional, and intellectual effort. And I have come to one conclusion: the highest goal of learning is to know God.

"But seek ye first the Kingdom of God, and His righteousness, and all these things shall be added unto you."

Matthew 6:33 (KJV)

March 2

An attitude of gratitude is necessary for attracting to ourselves more of what we already have and other things that we may desire. But three things prevent us from practicing and experiencing this attitude: Fault finding, complaining and grumbling, and a propensity to take what we have for granted. Stop complaining and grumbling. Replace these with thanksgiving and praise.

_____
_____
_____
_____
_____
_____
_____
_____
_____
_____
_____

"And do not grumble."

1 Corinthians 10:10 (NIV)

March 3

From today, start to commit to the most excellent and highest possible standards in all you do. Refuse to be content with mediocrity. Instead, commit to the perfect finish. Determine that whatever you set your hands upon will be built to last. Affirm to yourself always: At my table, only the best is good enough.

_____

_____
_____
_____
_____
_____
_____
_____
_____
_____
_____
_____

"And whatsoever ye do, do it heartily, as to the Lord, and not unto men."

Colossians 3:23 (KJV)

March 4

A person who is totally wrapped up in himself makes a pitifully small package. Start to include others in your plans.

_____
_____
_____
_____
_____
_____
_____
_____
_____
_____
_____
_____
_____
_____

"Each of you should look not only to your own interests, but also to the interests of others."

Philippians 2:4 (NIV)

March 5

"No one can make you inferior without your consent."

Eleanor Roosevelt
Former First Lady of the United States

Quite true. After all, you are a unique individual. No one is quite like you in any way. Even your fingerprints are unique to you, and you alone. So are your gifts and talents. Envy no one. Feel inferior to no one. You are simply one of a kind.

_____

_____

_____

_____

_____

_____

_____

_____

_____

"I will praise thee, for I am fearfully and wonderfully made."

Psalm 139:14 (KJV)

March 6

The best pictures of you are yet to be taken. The best stories about you are yet to be told. The best of your years still lie ahead. So, affirm to yourself today: "The good days are here, but the best is yet to come."

_____

_____

_____

_____

_____

_____

_____

_____

_____

_____

_____

_____

_____

"Your sun will never set again, and your moon will wane no more, the Lord will be your everlasting light, and your days of sorrow will end."

Isaiah 60:20 (NIV)

March 7

Resolve today to forgive everyone who has ever offended you in any way. You see, forgiveness is the key to the kingdom of inner peace. It's the hardest, yet the most important thing you'll ever do. It will set you free from the past, and yet also free up your mind for the germination of divine creativity.

_____

_____

_____

_____

_____

_____

_____

_____

_____

"Then Peter came to Jesus and asked, Lord, how many times shall I forgive my brother when he sins against me? Up to seven times? Jesus answered, I tell you, not seven times, but seventy times seven."

Matthew 18:21, 22 (NIV)

March 8

"Be sure that as you scramble up the ladder of success, it is leaning against the right wall."

Stephen Covey
The 7 Habits of Highly Effective People

This assertion is absolutely valid. As you crave and seek success, your motivation must derive from the correct value system and the proper belief pattern. Also, your goals must be ones you set for yourself, and not ones set for you by someone else.

_____
_____
_____
_____
_____
_____
_____
_____

"Above all else, guard your heart, for it is the wellspring of life."

Proverbs 4:23

March 9

All good things come to those who strive with patience. Dripping water, in time, will cut a hole through stone. As surely as the mystery of a giant tree lies dormant within a tiny seed, so is persistence, that winner's quality of holding on despite defeat upon defeat. In fact, persistence is self-discipline in action, since it's actually the real measure of your belief in yourself and your ability to succeed. Ultimately, persistence is the true measure of individual human character.

_____

_____

_____

_____

_____

_____

_____

_____

_____

_____

"But if we hope for that we see not, then do we with patience wait for it."

Romans 8:25 (KJV)

March 10

Pause for a moment, and take stock of your life right now. Anywhere and everywhere you turn, there are problems confronting you. Is this not true? Well, it is only an apparent truth. The real and salient truth is this: So many open doors of opportunity are inviting you in. It's just that these doors are disguised as all these seemingly intractable problems. Lucky you!

_____
_____
_____
_____
_____
_____
_____
_____
_____
_____

"I know your deeds. See, I have placed before you an open door that no one can shut."

Revelation 3:8 (NIV)

March 11

Affirm to yourself today: "I am afraid of nothing. I am afraid for nothing. God has conferred on me all wisdom, all power, all strength, and all understanding. There is no stopping me."

"Nay, in all these things we are more than conquerors through him that loved us."

Romans 8:37 (KJV)

March 12

The New Webster's Dictionary defines the word "best" as "something of the finest quality." Today, I invite you to write out the word "best" on a piece of paper, look at it continually, and celebrate it. Then do three things. Resolve to think only the best thoughts, contrive to work only for the best results, and entertain only the best expectations.

_____
_____
_____
_____
_____
_____
_____
_____
_____
_____

"Finally, brothers, whatever is true, whatever is noble, whatever is right, whatever is pure, whatever is lovely, whatever is admirable—if anything is excellent or praiseworthy—think about such things."

Ephesians 4:8 (NIV)

March 13

Once, I was introduced to a prominent, very successful businessman. He was about seventy-five years old, but he looked not a day older than fifty years. I asked him for his secret of youth. This is what he said: "Doctor, I have a special grace. Whenever I'm irritated or provoked, instead of flying into a rage, I fly into a great calm. I have disciplined myself not to get angry or resentful. I now have a depth of inner peace that nothing and nobody can disturb."

_____
_____
_____
_____
_____
_____
_____
_____
_____
_____

"When he giveth quietness, who then can make trouble."

Job 34:29 (KJV)

March 14

*"Leaders think and talk about solutions.
Followers think and talk about problems."*

Brian Tracy

How true this is. From today, resolve to never spend more than 10% of your time on the problem. Rather, decide to spend 90% of your time on the solution. This is the proactive way.

"That your love may abound more and more in knowledge and depth of insight, so that you may be able to discern what is best."

Philippians 1:9–10 (NIV)

March 15

I have always been aware of the relationship between ability and performance. I'm sure, so have you. However, I was fascinated to no end, and astonished by no small measure, when I became familiar with the real relationship between ability and performance. Small differences in your ability can lead to large differences in your performance. This, in management parlance, is called the "winning edge" concept.

_____

_____

_____

_____

_____

_____

_____

_____

_____

_____

"If the axe is dull and its edge unsharpened, more strength is needed but skill will bring success."

Ecclesiastes 10:10 (NIV)

March 16

The story is told of a farmer who had a propensity for expressing extreme negativity at all times. His neighbor dropped by to greet him.

Neighbor: "Congratulations! I hear you've had the biggest harvest in ten years!"

Farmer (looking very gloomy): "Well, it wasn't bad. But you see, a bumper harvest takes a lot out of the soil."

Often, we tend to focus on the negatives, rather than the positives, of life. Each time you catch yourself grumbling, think of those who have less. Refuse to complain.

_____

_____

_____

_____

_____

"And when the people complained, it displeased the Lord, and the Lord heard it, and His anger was kindled."

Numbers 11:1 (KJV)

March 17

"If you cannot fly, run. If you cannot run, walk. If you cannot walk, crawl. By all means, keep moving. Don't ever give up."

Martin Luther King

_____
_____
_____
_____
_____
_____
_____
_____
_____
_____
_____

"Do everything without complaining and arguing."

Philippians 2:14 (NIV)

March 18

Today, so many matters will crave your valuable attention. The urgent, and the not so urgent. Those things that matter, and those that do not matter. By and large, as usual, you will be as busy as a bee. But consider this: What does it matter how much you are doing if what you are doing is not what matters most? Always ask yourself: What is the most valuable use of my time right now?

_____

_____

_____

_____

_____

_____

_____

_____

_____

_____

"Redeeming the time, because the days are evil."

Ephesians 5:16 (KJV)

March 19

The times were very harrowing and traumatic for Dele Smith. He went to see his pastor.

Dele Smith: *"I have invited God into the picture as you advised me to do. But He has remained silent. I'm at my tether's end."*

Pastor: *"Patience, Smith, patience! Is it not a wise teacher that maintains silence and a thoughtful smile while his student, on his own, draws insightful conclusions?"*

Dele Smith: *"I ... I ... don't understand."*

Pastor: *"God teaches patience by His silence. And it is in this furnace of patience that hope is forged. Faith comes by hearing, but patience comes by God's absolute silence. Just as patience keeps the marathon racer from collapsing, so does patience serve as a soothing balm for your tormented soul."*

"And not only so, but we glory in tribulations also, knowing that tribulation worketh patience."

Romans 5:3 (KJV)

March 20

Wisdom is a rather complex word, isn't it? You can turn it inside out, like you would do to a shirt, and you would still be left with the same meaning. For after all, wisdom is learning all you can, and then having the humility to realize that you don't know it all.

_____

_____

_____

_____

_____

_____

_____

_____

_____

_____

_____

_____

"Happy is the man that findeth wisdom, and the man that getteth understanding."

Proverbs 3:13 (KJV)

March 21

From today, simply decide to become a detached observer of life. The reason for this is quite simple. Everything and everyone around you is your teacher.

"Submitting yourselves one to another in the fear of God."

Ephesians 5:21 (KJV)

March 22

Without an iota of doubt, the quality of your life will be determined by how much you do the right thing for the right reason in the right manner at the right time.

_____

_____

_____

_____

_____

_____

_____

_____

_____

_____

_____

_____

"Then you will understand what is right and just and fair—every good path."

Proverbs 2:9 (NIV)

March 23

Compassion is a commonly used word. The scope of its meaning and application goes beyond mere kindness. Its expression is a reflection of the potential bigness of the human heart. It involves the willingness to do four things: Put yourself in someone else's shoes, take the focus off of yourself, imagine what it's like to be in someone else's predicament, and then feel love for that person.

_____

_____

_____

_____

_____

_____

_____

_____

"But a certain Samaritan, as he journeyed, came where he was, and when he saw him, he had compassion on him. And went to him, and bound up his wounds, pouring in oil and wine, and set him on his own beast, and brought him to an inn, and took care of him."

Luke 10:33–34 (KJV)

March 24

No one can quite achieve his full potential by doing it or going it all alone. Start to network with others. Become a team player. For truly, we are better together than we are alone—this is called synergy.

_____
_____
_____
_____
_____
_____
_____
_____
_____
_____
_____
_____

"From him the whole body, joined and held together by every supporting ligament, grows and builds itself up in love, as each part does its work."

Ephesians 4:16 (NIV)

March 25

Affirm to yourself today:
"I expect my every need to be met.
I expect the answer to every problem.
I expect abundance on every level."

_____

_____

_____

_____

_____

_____

_____

_____

_____

_____

"In my Father's house are many mansions, if it were not so, I would have told you. I go to prepare a place for you."

John 14:2 (NIV)

March 26

"Without faith, you are helpless in the School of Signs and Wonders, a School which can also be called the School of the Miraculous, or the School of the Supernatural. It takes faith to command the supernatural, and it takes faith to receive its blessings when it is being administered."

Bishop David O. Oyedepo

_____

_____

_____

_____

_____

_____

_____

_____

_____

"Verily, Verily, I say unto you, He that believeth on me, the works that I do shall he do also, and greater works than these shall he do, because I go unto my father."

John 14:12 (KJV)

March 27

Of all creation, man was created as a master, to dominate and subdue the Earth. This is because God has put in man a part of Himself that allows man to conquer his environment. Conversely, you were not made to bow to circumstances and travails, but to subdue them. So, know today that you are meant to shine like gold. Like the stars.

_____

_____

_____

_____

_____

_____

_____

_____

_____

_____

"All kinds of animals, birds, reptiles and creatures of the sea are being tamed and have been tamed by man."

James 3:7 (NIV)

March 28

"The death of a seed is the burial of a forest."

Dr. Myles Munroe

Sow a seed today. Devise all sorts of offerings. This is most conveniently done by tying your offerings to one thing or the other. Then give willingly. You see, the financial seed you sow today may leave your hand, but it will never leave your life. So, always remember, if you keep your seed, that is the most it will be. But if you sow your seed, that is the least it will be.

"While the earth remaineth, seedtime and harvest, and cold and heat, and summer and winter, and day and night shall not cease."

Genesis 8:22 (KJV)

March 29

While being coached for the Common Entrance Examination in the early 1970s, I was taught to tackle the easier questions first, so as to have sufficient time for the more difficult questions. We should adopt the same strategy in facing life's challenges. Start with the simple challenges. Tougher challenges consume more time, discourage you, confuse you, and make you rush through the rest. Worse still, your finishing may turn out quite faulty.

"Therefore, I do not run like a man running aimlessly; I do not fight like a man beating the air."

1 Corinthians 9:26 (NIV)

March 30

It's incredible, isn't it? Ours is such a consumer-based economy; we are so busy consuming that we seem to neglect our capacity to produce. What can you produce to fill some human need, and for which you can expect your own share of Gods' material abundance?

_____

_____

_____

_____

_____

_____

_____

_____

_____

_____

_____

_____

_____

"A great door for effective work has opened to me."

1 Corinthians 16:9 (NIV)

March 31

Today is the last day in the first quarter of the year. Take time to celebrate your successes, and even your failures, so far. Give thanks and simply allow yourself to become mesmerized by the graciousness of God and the magic of it all.

_____

_____

_____

_____

_____

_____

_____

_____

_____

_____

_____

_____

"The Lord hath done great things for us; whereof we are glad."

Psalms 126:3 (KJV)

April 1

Today is the first of April, April Fool's Day, and on this same day, a man smashed into a parked car outside a busy shopping mall. A minute later, he got out and placed a note under the windshield wiper of the damaged car. Then, he drove off. An hour later, the owner arrived and saw the damage to his car. But then, he also saw the note, on which was written: "I have just run into your car. Many people saw it happen and are watching me. They think I'm leaving my name and number. I'm not! I've April fooled them!"

Well, one thing is certain. This man's conscience will indict him. Refuse to overload your conscience. Live your life as if it were spent in a stadium filled with spectators.

_____

_____

_____

_____

_____

"For nothing is secret, that shall not be made manifest, neither anything hid that shall not be known and come abroad."

Luke 8:17 (KJV)

April 2

Michael Subomi Balogun was the first Nigerian to be given a license to set up a bank without the necessity of foreign technical partners.

In the lobby of Primrose Tower, headquarters of his First City Group, is a plaque on which is written all that the man stands for:

"This block, Primrose Tower, is dedicated to the glory of God as an embodiment of a young man's faith in the unfailing support of the Almighty God and in his own destiny, in spite of the seeming insurmountable obstacles. It is also a monument of a young man's determination to succeed and to prove that, given the opportunity, he has the mettle to attain the commanding heights in the management of a finance institution. Lastly, it serves as a lesson to all mankind that in all things, mortals may have their say, but in the final analysis, the Almighty God will have His way."

How you cope with adversity and challenge will shape your life more than almost anything else.

"But we glory in tribulations also, knowing that tribulation worketh patience, and patience experience, and experience, hope."

Romans 5:3-4 (KJV)

April 3

The characterization and assessment of a person is not usually as simple as people generally think, and it can be quite as complex as human nature itself. Many words can describe a person, but three of them stand out: reputation, personality and character.

Your reputation is what everyone thinks you are.

Your personality is what you seem to be.

Your character is what you really are.

_____

_____

_____

_____

_____

_____

_____

"A good name is more desirable than great riches, to be esteemed is better than silver or gold."

Proverbs 22:1 (NIV)

April 4

Life is a great challenge. This is a great truth. But once you truly understand and accept this truth, the fact that life is such a great challenge no longer matters. Then life becomes an infinitely easier project to pursue.

_____
_____
_____
_____
_____
_____
_____
_____
_____
_____
_____
_____

"Behold, I am the Lord, the God of all flesh, is there anything too hard for me?"

Jeremiah 32:27 (KJV)

April 5

To be a high-achiever, you must develop and possess a trait called "response-ability." This is the ability to take both credit and blame for all that happens to you. Being responsible for all your actions and inactions, you refuse to blame anyone and anything. You take full responsibility for your situation. Whatever it is, you probably got yourself into it in the first place. Even if it's not your fault, you are still responsible for your response. This way, you will become the master of your fate and the captain of your soul.

_____
_____
_____
_____
_____
_____
_____
_____
_____

"And if I do what I do not want to do, I agree that the law is good."

Romans 7:16 (NIV)

April 6

The only thing that stands between you and what you want is the will to try and the faith to believe that it is possible. How do you know you can't when you haven't even tried?

_____

_____

_____

_____

_____

_____

_____

_____

_____

_____

_____

_____

_____

"I tell you the truth, if you have faith as small as a mustard seed, you can say to this mountain, move from here to there and it will move. Nothing will be impossible for you."

Matthew 17:21 (NIV)

April 7

If you wake up in the morning and can think of nothing but writing, then you are a writer. If you wake up and can think of nothing but flying a plane, then you are potentially a pilot. On the other hand, if you wake up and can think of nothing but singing, then you are a singer. If that is so, why are you not singing? It would be simply tragic for you to go to your grave with your music still inside you.

"We have different gifts, according to the grace given us."

Romans 12:6 (NIV)

April 8

Someone gave a dog a fine, meaty bone. With the bone firmly between his teeth, he trotted home happily. He had to cross a bridge. Reaching the middle of the bridge, he glanced down into the water and saw his own reflection magnified. Thinking the other dog had a bigger bone, the dog decided to take it forcefully. He leaned over and snapped at his own reflection. As he did so, the bone in his mouth fell into the water. He lost it.

_____

_____

_____

_____

_____

_____

_____

_____

"And he said unto them, take heed, and beware of covetousness; for a man's life consisteth not in the abundance of the things which he possesseth."

Luke 12:15 (KJV)

April 9

Affirm to yourself today;
"I am a unique individual with a unique personality and a unique
purpose in life. I am an original."

_____

_____

_____

_____

_____

_____

_____

_____

_____

_____

_____

_____

"I have glorified thee on the earth; I have finished the work which
thou gavest me to do."

John 17:4 (KJV)

April 10

Always look for the good in every situation. Develop the mindset that every setback is part of a great plan, a conspiracy if you like, that is moving you toward the success that is inevitably yours. In other words, become an inverse optimist. This means that at every turn, the whole world is in a conspiracy to do you good.

_____
_____
_____
_____
_____
_____
_____
_____
_____
_____
_____
_____
_____

"Surely it was for my benefit that I suffered such anguish."

Isaiah 38:17 (NIV)

April 11

Recognizing that genius is simply the ability to do the common thing uncommonly well, successful people are usually quite thorough, even to minute detail. Realizing that little things can mean a lot, they don't take chances and take nothing for granted.

"In the eleventh year in the month of Bul, the eighth month, the temple was finished in all its details according to its specifications. He had spent seven years building it."

1 Kings 6:38 (NIV)

April 12

The story is told of a wealthy and successful South African building contractor who would refuse to sign any contract until this statement was added at the end of the page: "In the presence of God Almighty." He was known to be an honorable businessman. How prepared are you to sign God's name to your own contract papers?

_____

_____

_____

_____

_____

_____

_____

_____

_____

_____

"And whatever you do, whether in word or deed, do it all in the name of the Lord Jesus, giving thanks to God the Father through Him."

Colossians 3:17 (NIV)

April 13

Respond to ideas and refuse to react to the person. Know that even a bitter enemy will say truths that need to be heard. Indeed, for all you know, even he may have been sent to you, to tell you the truth.

"For it will not be you speaking but the spirit of your Father speaking through you."

Matthew 10:20 (NIV)

April 14

My daughter, a pretty young lady in her early teens, combines a strong intellectual bent with an amazing proclivity for misplacing things on such a consistent basis that I've often wondered if there is a relationship between the two traits. Anyway, my prescription to her, which is beginning to sound like a broken record, is this:

"Order is the first law of heaven. A place for everything; and everything in its place."

Happily, she's beginning to respond to treatment.

_____

_____

_____

_____

_____

_____

_____

_____

"Let all things be done decently and in order."

1 Corinthians 14:40 (KJV)

April 15

A man is a fool who can't be angry. But a man is wise who won't be angry. He who conquers his anger is a spiritual four-star general. He has conquered a great enemy indeed.

"A fool gives full vent to his anger, but a wise man keeps himself under control."

Proverbs 29:11 (NIV)

April 16

"God, grant me the serenity to accept the things I cannot change, the courage to change the things I can, and the wisdom to know the difference."

The Serenity Prayer

"Wisdom makes one wise man more powerful than ten rulers in a city."

Ecclesiastes 7:19 (NIV)

April 17

To be a visionary leader, you must develop the ability to think very far into the future while making decisions in the present. This means that your main business is both to see what lies dimly at a distance and also to do what lies clearly at hand.

"*Let your eyes look straight ahead, fix your gaze directly before you.*"

Proverbs 4:25 (NIV)

April 18

Refuse to capitalize on your gains. Anyone can do that. The important thing is to profit from your losses. That requires a certain degree of intelligence.

_____

_____

_____

_____

_____

_____

_____

_____

_____

_____

_____

_____

_____

"If any man's work shall be burned, he shall suffer loss; but he himself shall be saved."

1 Corinthians 3:15 (KJV)

April 19

"Jack of all trades, master of none." This translates to: Concentrate your energy. To be everywhere is to be nowhere. Today affirm to yourself:

"I am concentrated, firmly grounded in the center of my being and nothing can distract me."

"My heart is fixed, O God, my heart is fixed: I will sing and give praise."

Psalm 57:7 (KJV)

April 20

Today, contemplate on this definition of peace of mind:

"Peace of mind is wealth without which you cannot really be wealthy."

_____
_____
_____
_____
_____
_____
_____
_____
_____
_____
_____
_____

"Thou wilt keep him in perfect peace, whose mind is stayed on thee, because he trusteth in thee."

Isaiah 26:3 (KJV)

April 21

In my country, Nigeria, "big man" connotes a position of power and affluence, especially in the view of the economically disadvantaged. But an uncle's steward defines "big man" differently. Hear him. "You can tell a big man by the way he treats little people. My boss is a big man. He's very kind to me."

_____

_____

_____

_____

_____

_____

_____

_____

_____

_____

_____

"The king asked, 'Is there no-one still left of the house of Saul to whom I can show God's kindness?'"

2 Samuel 9:3 (NIV)

April 22

"The fox is clever because he knows many things; but the tortoise is smarter because he knows one big thing!"

Nigerian folktale

_____

_____

_____

_____

_____

_____

_____

_____

_____

_____

_____

_____

"The heart of the prudent getteth knowledge; and the ear of the wise seeketh knowledge."

Proverbs 18:15 (KJV)

April 23

Good sense and desire have a curious relationship. Those in whom good sense overpowers desire tend to flourish and have peace of mind. Those, however, in whom desire overpowers good sense tend to get into serious trouble.

"I have learned the secret of being content in any and every situation, whether well fed or hungry, whether living in plenty or in want."

Philippians 4:12 (NIV)

April 24

An old miser sold all he had and bought a big lump of gold that he buried in the ground, visiting the site every day to look at the gold. His servant, observing his frequent visits, spied on him, discovered his secret, and crept back later to steal the gold. The next day, the miser found an empty hole and became extremely distraught with grief. His best friend in consoling him, said, "Stop crying. Get a stone of equal size. Paint it a golden color and bury it. Each day visit it and pretend that your gold is still there. The stone will serve the same purpose, since you never meant to use the gold anyway."

"I have seen a grievous evil under the sun. Wealth hoarded to the harm of its owner."

Ecclesiastes 5:13 (NIV)

April 25

I have always been, both on the spiritual and intellectual levels, fascinated by what I have come to personally characterize as the Triad of Excellence: faith, love, and hope. It would seem that a common thread binds them together: inspiration. The way I see it is this:

Faith opens the doorway to inspiration.

Hope powers the forward thrust of inspiration.

Love gives divine direction to inspiration.

"And now these three remain: faith, hope and love. But the greatest of these is love."

1 Corinthians 13:13 (NIV)

April 26

Wouldn't it be ridiculous if you committed some act of wrong doing and then went ahead to glorify your misdeed?

Well, the same thought should apply to doing good. Put in other words, making a big deal out of doing good is like making a big deal out of doing wrong. So, today, do a kind deed for someone secretly and make sure you are not found out. Let it remain a secret.

_____

_____

_____

_____

_____

_____

_____

_____

_____

_____

"But when you give to the needy, do not let your left hand know what your right hand is doing, so that your giving may be in secret."

Matthew 6:3–4 (NIV)

April 27

Tunde Martins (not his real names) is a compulsive gambler. A wealthy young man, he regularly and sporadically takes time off his business to register his presence at the casinos of Monte Carlo, Las Vegas, and London. He is very proud of his gambling skills and boasts that he "deals one of the best hands" around.

What's the point in doing well that which you should not be doing at all? Examine yourself. Are you doing what you think it best to do and avoiding what you think it best to avoid?

_____

_____

_____

_____

_____

_____

_____

_____

"Thus saith the Lord of hosts; consider your ways."

Haggai 1:7 (KJV)

April 28

An out-of-work, secondary school dropout was accused of raping a twelve-year-old girl. He readily admitted to the offence but attempted a feeble defense that the devil tempted him. The judge, who also happened to be a lay preacher in the church, replied: "The devil tempts all. Quite true. But an idle man tempts the devil."

_____

_____

_____

_____

_____

_____

_____

_____

_____

_____

"When tempted, no one should say, 'God is tempting me.' For God cannot be tempted by evil, nor does He tempt anyone; but each one is tempted when, by his own evil desire, he is dragged away and enticed."

James 1:13–14 (NIV)

April 29

Time: that very essence of life; the most valuable perishable commodity on earth. Because it slips through our hands like grains of sand, never to return again, its wise use usually leads to a rich and productive life. Conversely, failure to appreciate its value and deploy it wisely will result in an aftermath of regret and loss. So, live this day as if it were your last. Continually ask yourself, "What is the most valuable use of my time right now?"

"I must work the works of Him that sent me, while it is day; the night cometh, when no man can work."

John 9:4 (KJV)

April 30

Trouble is an inevitability in our lives. When it comes, hold up your head high, look it squarely in the eye and say, "I am bigger than you. You cannot defeat me."

_____
_____
_____
_____
_____
_____
_____
_____
_____
_____
_____
_____
_____
_____

"Yet man is born unto trouble, as the sparks fly upward."

Job 5:7 (KJV)

May 1

Today is worker's day and it's a day set aside all over the world by trade unions to celebrate the labor and sweat of the working man. If you are an employer of labor, resolve today to encourage your workers to render more and better service, so that you will be naturally motivated to give them more and bigger responsibilities, which will in turn lead to more and better wages.

"The labourer is worthy of his reward."

1 Timothy 5:18 (KJV)

May 2

Guard your firmness with a little bit of flexibility. Refuse to be too rigid in your ways and views. Likewise, preserve your strength with some weakness.

Remember, the thin, flexible reed by the river bank that bends over backward to accommodate the strong wind stands a greater chance of survival than the thick, rigid oak tree in the face of the same strong wind.

_____
_____
_____
_____
_____
_____
_____
_____
_____

"And he said unto me, my grace is sufficient for thee, for my strength is made perfect in weakness."

2 Corinthians 12:9 (KJV)

May 3

Advance fee fraudsters are on the prowl, looking for the next gullible victim. When the man with money meets the man with experience, the man with money is usually left with the experience, while the man with experience leaves with the money. Guard your hard-earned money well. Refuse to lose it to any hare-brained scheme.

"Watch out that you do not lose what you have worked for, but that you may be rewarded fully."

2 John 8 (NIV)

May 4

"Your best friend is the one who brings out the best in you."

Henry Ford

_____

_____

_____

_____

_____

_____

_____

_____

_____

_____

_____

_____

"Iron sharpeneth iron, so a man sharpeneth the countenance of his friend."

Proverbs 27:17 (KJV)

May 5

A man was out of job and had only one loaf of bread left. In great despondence, he took a rope and headed for the forest. His mission: to commit suicide. At a clearing in the forest, he saw a blind, one-legged man dancing and singing praises to the Lord.

Out-of-job man: *"Why are you so happy? What's there to make you happy?"*

Happy man: *"I just discovered that I still have half a loaf of bread left. Isn't life simply great? And God simply good?"*

Out-of-job man bowed his head in shame and traced his way back home to give thanks for his complete body, good health, and one loaf of bread.

_____

_____

_____

_____

_____

"In everything give thanks."

1 Thessalonians 5:18 (KJV)

May 6

Consider this very carefully. Has it occurred to you that what's holding you back may not be a lack of resources? Could it conceivably be that your major drawback is rather a lack of resourcefulness?

Pray that God may grant you the grace to become a creative reservoir of profitable ideas. Consider how these people creatively gained access to Jesus.

_____

_____

_____

_____

_____

_____

_____

_____

"Since they could not get him to Jesus because of the crowd, they made an opening in the roof above Jesus and, after digging through it, lowered the mat the paralyzed man was lying on."

Mark 2:4 (NIV)

May 7

"I have chosen to focus on the front windshield and not on the rear-view mirror of life"

Gen. Colin Powell
Former American Secretary of State
Former Chairman, Joint Chiefs of Staff

There is always something in our past that we regret. It could be an honest mistake or even a foolish, misguided decision. We wish it had not happened. Well, the past will always remain a part of your life, but it doesn't have to determine your future. Resolve today to focus on the future with hope and enthusiasm.

_____

_____

_____

_____

_____

_____

_____

"For a just man falleth several times, and riseth up again."

Proverbs 24:16 (KJV)

May 8

"Usually, things turn out the best for those who make the best of the way things turn out."

Zig Ziglar

This is very true. Those who make the best of any situation, no matter how potentially bad, are those who are armed with an attitude of positive expectations and inverse optimism. They have this consistent belief that the whole world, at every turn, is conspiring to do them good. For them, in every adversity lies the seed of an equal or greater opportunity.

_____

_____

_____

_____

_____

_____

_____

"But those who hope in the Lord will renew their strength."

Isaiah 40:31 (NIV)

May 9

Much of life's failures are caused by wrong decisions. In our lives, we have to make a series of decisions, each of seemingly little consequence. Yet, the sum total of all these decisions determines the final outcome of our life. A successful life depends upon developing a higher percentage of wisdom than error. In arriving at a decision, a businessman friend of mine employs a simple formula:

- *Is it ethically right?*
- *Is it absolutely fair to all concerned?*
- *Is it based on what is right, rather than who is right?*
- *Will it do the most for the most?*

"But the wisdom that comes from heaven is first of all pure; then peace-loving, considerate, submissive, full of mercy and good fruit, impartial and sincere."

James 3:17 (NIV)

May 10

Today, take a trip into fantasy land. Indulge your imagination and visualize that your life is perfect in every conceivable way. What does it look like? Assuming a conformity, on your part, to God's will, visualizing in this manner will allow you to align perfectly with His plan and purpose for your life.

_____

_____

_____

_____

_____

_____

_____

_____

_____

_____

_____

"Your sun will never set again, and your moon will wane no more, the Lord will be your everlasting light, and your days of sorrow will end."

Isaiah 60:20 (NIV)

May 11

Good health is based on natural principles. It results from regular exercise, proper diet, adequate rest, the proper mental attitude, the proper spiritual diet, and the avoidance of harmful substances. Take adequate care of your body, and your body will take adequate care of you.

_____

_____

_____

_____

_____

_____

_____

_____

_____

_____

_____

"Know ye not that ye are the temple of God, and that the spirit of God dwelleth in you?"

1 Corinthians 3:16 (KJV)

May 12

Do you welcome Monday mornings with open arms, and with joy in your heart? Many of us don't. This is because many of us don't like what we do for a living. If you don't love your job, how can you possibly make a success of it?

Make sure that you are doing what brings joy to your heart. Then you can affirm to yourself, "I love what I do, and I do what I love."

"Whatever you do, work at it with all your heart, as working for the Lord, not for men."

Colossians 3:23 (NIV)

May 13

"It does not matter where you are coming from. All that matters is where you are going."

Ancient Greek philosophy

Meditate very deeply on this statement.

"Remember ye not the former things, neither consider the things of old."

Isaiah 43:18 (KJV)

May 14

Sometime in late 2005, at the airport in Lagos, I sighted a man I had long admired but never met. He is your quintessential captain of industry. He is chairman of seven companies and sits on the boards of ten others. For me, he was a role model of sorts. As is my habit, I walked up to him and we got talking. It turned out his life had not always been a bed of roses. We talked for an hour. I quote his parting words to me:

"Success is actually failure turned inside out. It's impossible for you to evolve into your full potential unless you face adversity and learn from it. Life's great victories come from overcoming defeats and setbacks. May your own road be rough enough for you to profit from its potholes and narrow bridges."

_____

_____

_____

_____

"But small is the gate and narrow the road that leads to life, and only few find it."

Matthew 7:14 (NIV)

May 15

Still on goals: Take your goals and plant them in the fertile soil of your imagination. If they blossom, pursue them. If on the other hand, they grow thorns, or wither and die, uproot them and plant other seeds.

_____

_____

_____

_____

_____

_____

_____

_____

_____

_____

"There are many devises in a man's heart; nevertheless the counsel of the Lord, that shall stand."

Proverbs 19:21 (KJV)

May 16

Fear no man!

_____
_____
_____
_____
_____
_____
_____
_____
_____
_____
_____
_____
_____
_____
_____

"The fear of man bringeth a snare, but whoso putteth his trust in the Lord shall be safe."

Proverbs 29:25 (KJV)

May 17

A couple, married now for all of thirty years, were out driving. She suddenly said, "You know dear, you are not as romantic as you used to be in the early days of our marriage. We used to sit close together when out driving, but now you sit so far away."

The husband replied gently, "My dear, I am sitting exactly where I always sit while driving. In the driver's seat."

Beware of a critical attitude. Apart from blinding you to your own faults, it can also backfire!

"You hypocrite, first take the plank out of your own eye, and then you will see clearly to remove the speck from your brother's eye."

Matthew 7:5 (NIV)

May 18

Our tendency to become anxious, perhaps even extremely so, in the face of uncertainty is a truly worrisome one. Its presence in some people can even be elevated to the psychiatric status of anxiety neurosis. Yet, anxiety does not empty tomorrow of its sorrows but only empties today of its strength, for the beginning of anxiety is the end of faith and the beginning of faith is the end of anxiety.

"Do not be anxious about anything, but in everything by prayer and petition, with thanksgiving, present your requests to God."

Philippians 4:6 (NIV)

May 19

You start to become great when you begin to listen to your inner voice. This inner witness is actually an inward impression on your heart—it is a subtle feeling, it is an intuitive feeling, and it is always right. Your conscience, which is akin to an internal policeman, speaks to you through this "still, small voice." Each person hears it differently. To some, it comes naturally. Others must cultivate it through the internal quietude that comes with meditation and contemplation. Either way, it is the Holy Spirit speaking to you.

"The spirit itself beareth witness with our spirit, that we are the children of God."

Romans 8:16 (KJV)

May 20

It is not the events in your life that shape you but your beliefs as to what those events mean. Actually, nothing in life has any meaning except the meaning you choose to give it.

"Meaningless! Meaningless!
Says the Teacher -
Utterly meaningless!
Everything is meaningless"

Ecclesiastes 1:2 (NIV)

May 21

Absolutely refuse to engage in gossip. Refuse to run the other person down. Button up your lips securely against words that hurt. Instead, be quick to utter words that comfort.

"Let no corrupt communication proceed out of your mouth, but that which is good to the use of edifying, that it may minister grace unto the heavens."

Ephesians 4:29 (KJV)

May 22

To maximize your life and potential, you have to minimize your load. You must determine what is important and worthy of your attention. You must focus your spiritual energy and refuse to spread it too thin. Actually, most things are not quite as important as you presume, and what you consider a crisis may be no more than a tempest in a teacup. Sit loosely in the saddle of life.

_____

_____

_____

_____

_____

_____

_____

_____

_____

_____

_____

"Make it your ambition to lead a quiet life."

1 Thessalonians 4:11 (NIV)

May 23

You are necessarily a daily decision maker. These decisions must be based on sound information and reliable data. That is why the people around you must be wise and competent. However, after listening, you must take the final decision, as you will be the person to live with the consequences.

"Where no counsel is, the people fall; but in the multitude of counsellors there is safety."

Proverbs 11:14 (KJV)

May 24

Anger is the most destructive of the negative emotions of man. It can be likened to an electric current. We may allow it to pass through us, but we should not hang onto it. Anger robs us of objectivity, especially in times when we need to maintain levelheadedness. Worse still, anger can fester into bitterness, that cancer of the soul. Eliminate anger from your life.

_____
_____
_____
_____
_____
_____
_____
_____
_____
_____

"Cease from anger, and forsake wrath, fret not thyself in any wise to do evil."

Psalm 37:8 (KJV)

May 25

John and Samuel were next-door neighbors on a quiet suburban street in Lagos. John woke up one morning to spot a gleaming, new model of the Toyota Camry in Samuel's garage. He went green with envy, and by the next day, he had the same brand of car in his own garage. He didn't know that Samuel's car was a gift from his wealthy father-in-law. John, on the other hand, had had to exhaust all his savings to buy his own car.

One good reason why envy and covetousness are such terrible afflictions is because what is right for others may not be right for you. If your motivation is to have what others have, your decisions will be targeted at the wrong or untimely goal. Your goal must be self-geared and not to keep up with the neighbors. Compare your self only with yourself.

"For where you have envy and selfish ambition, there you find disorder and every evil practice."

James 3:16 (NIV)

May 26

Most of us live lives of near-desperate, constant physical and mental agitation. We seem to believe that frenetic, fire-brigade activity is synonymous with effectiveness. How tragic! We could learn a lot from the Japanese. Japan is now one of the most industrialized nations on earth, yet the Japanese consistently maintain a dignified calm and tranquility in all they do. In fact, the practice of quietness has been elevated to art form in Japan. It is called ryomi.

_____

_____

_____

_____

_____

_____

_____

_____

_____

_____

_____

"In quietness and in confidence shall be your strength."

Isaiah 30:15 (KJV)

May 27

Today is celebrated the world over as Children's Day. Take time off today to think very deeply about your child. The four needs of your child are as follows:

- Spiritual needs
- Emotional needs
- Physical needs
- Academic needs

Review how far you have gone in meeting these needs of your child, but most importantly, train up that child in the way he should go, and be sure to go that way yourself!

_____
_____
_____
_____
_____
_____

"Bring them up in the training and instruction of the Lord."

Ephesians 4:6 (NIV)

May 28

Today, let us play around with the two words efficiency and effectiveness. The two words are so closely related that one shouldn't be amazed at the seeming confusion generated in their commonplace usage. Efficiency is the ability to do something well without wasted energy or effort, whilst to be effective is simply to do something well.

_____

_____

_____

_____

_____

_____

_____

_____

_____

_____

_____

_____

"Because a great door for effective work has opened to me."

1 Corinthians 16:9 (NIV)

May 29

You don't have to be great to start, but you do have to start to become great. If you have a rather big goal, today take the biggest possible step in the direction of its fulfillment. If the step looks relatively tiny, do not worry if it's the biggest possible for now.

_____

_____

_____

_____

_____

_____

_____

_____

_____

_____

"Being confident of this, that He who began a good work in you will carry it on to completion."

Philippians 1:6 (NIV)

May 30

If a book titled, "A Synopsis of Successful Living," were to be written, it would, in all probability, contain the following five chapters:

- Identify your talents. (Use them to glorify God, and to benefit humanity.)
- Have faith. (In the favor of God.)
- Engage in proper planning.
- 10% belongs to God.
- Give, give, and keep on giving.

_____

_____

_____

_____

_____

_____

_____

"But just as you excel in everything—in faith, in speech, in knowledge, in complete earnestness and in your love for us—see that you also excel in this grace of giving."

2 Corinthians 8:7 (NIV)

May 31

Refuse to be a loser. Losers visualize the penalties of failure. Rather, absolutely insist on being a winner. Winners visualize the rewards of success. It cannot be otherwise, since winners have God on their side.

_____

_____

_____

_____

_____

_____

_____

_____

_____

_____

_____

_____

"What shall we then say to these things? If God be for us, who can be against us?"

Romans 8:31 (KJV)

June 1

Simply refuse to hold a grudge against anyone. You cannot develop upper level personality if you allow yourself to collect and hold grievances. Besides, and perhaps on a more mundane level, while you are preoccupied with the grudge you are holding against some people, they are out dancing, totally oblivious of your negative feelings toward them.

"Do not seek revenge or bear a grudge against one of your people, but love your neighbour as yourself. I am the Lord."

Leviticus 19:18 (NIV)

June 2

On graduation day, a young man was presented with a Bible by his wealthy father. Angrily, he flung the Bible down, stormed out of the house, and out of his father's life. Thirty years later, he returned home for the burial of his father, who had willed his entire estate to him. He found the Bible still lying on his father's table, and tearfully opened it to find that his father had underlined Matthew 7:11. At the same time, a car key dropped from the back of the Bible. It was for a sports car he had wanted as a graduation gift thirty years earlier.

Indeed, how many times do we miss our blessings because they are not packaged as we expected?

_____

_____

_____

_____

"If you, then, though you are evil, know how to give good gifts to your children, how much more will your father in heaven give good gifts to those who ask him!"

Matthew 7:11 (NIV)

June 3

You possess a spark of individual brilliance that is unique to you and you alone. Indeed, you are intrinsically capable of accomplishing something in your own peculiar way that cannot be replicated by anyone else. Life has not been playing hide and seek with you. Rather, you've been blind. Your unique abilities have displayed themselves in many situations. It's just that you've been so focused on making a living that you saw nothing else.

_____

_____

_____

_____

_____

_____

_____

_____

_____

"Each one should use whatever gift he has received to serve others, faithfully administering God's grace in its various forms."

1 Peter 4:10 (NIV)

June 4

You must have a clear vision of what you want. A mere dream of what you want is not adequate. Instead, cultivate a desire so strong and a vision so clear that they become fully embedded in your subconscious mind, which, it would seem, is especially receptive to your deeper aspirations and values.

_____

_____

_____

_____

_____

_____

_____

_____

_____

_____

_____

"And all Judah rejoiced at the oath, for they had sworn with all their heart, and sought him with their whole desire."

2 Chronicles 15:15 (KJV)

June 5

If you focus exclusively on the shortcomings of the people with whom you have to relate and forget that they have good points, it will be difficult, if not near impossible, to find good and worthy people in all this world.

_____

_____

_____

_____

_____

_____

_____

_____

_____

_____

_____

"For there is not a just man upon earth, that doeth good, and sinneth not. Also take no heed unto all words that are spoken, lest thou hear thy servant curse thee."

Ecclesiastes 7:20–21 (KJV)

June 6

There was once a very wise king. Whenever he paid a royal visit to a land where all the people went about naked, he would take off all his clothes as he entered the land, and put them back on when he left.

"I, wisdom, dwell together with prudence;
I possess knowledge and discretion."
"By me kings reign,
And rulers make laws that are just."

Proverbs 8:12, 15 (NIV)

June 7

My nephew was in an interview for a job. In his CV, he had listed his pastor, home cell leader, and a deacon as his referees. The interviewer, after a careful scrutiny of the CV, said: "I appreciate and commend you for these recommendations from your church. But I'd still like to hear from your weekday acquaintances."

This request should be considered perfectly valid and in order. For after all, the principles you practice on Sundays should be in accord with those you practice on weekdays. Refuse to live by a double standard.

"They could find no corruption in him, because he was trustworthy and neither corrupt nor negligent."

Daniel 6:4 (NIV)

June 8

Do much for yourself, but even more for others. This supreme devotion to your fellow human being will endow you with great power. You will ordinarily appear to be the smallest, most insignificant, and most modest of men. But, in reality, you will be among the greatest of men.

_____

_____

_____

_____

_____

_____

_____

_____

_____

_____

_____

"Do nothing out of selfish ambition or vain conceit, but in humility consider others better than yourselves. Each of you should look not only to your own interests, but also to the interests of others."

Philippians 2:3–4 (NIV)

June 9

Today, commit yourself to setting that goal of moving into your own home next year. Pick a pen and a piece of paper, and write. "I complete my own home and move into it next year, 2009." But you still have to improve on this. You must set a deadline for the achievement of this goal. So, pick the pen and write: "I complete my own home and move into it on 17 December 2009." Now, that's better. The purpose of this exercise is simply this. It is to teach us that a real goal, one that we are serious about, is different from a wish. A goal is clear, written, specific, and has a deadline for its achievement. A goal without a deadline is merely a discussion.

"Forgetting what is behind and straining towards what is ahead, I press on towards the goal."

Philippians 3:13–14 (NIV)

June 10

"Faith is to believe what you do not see. The reward of this faith is to see what you believe."

St. Augustine

_____
_____
_____
_____
_____
_____
_____
_____
_____
_____
_____

"By faith, Abraham, when called to go to a place he would later receive as his inheritance, obeyed and went, even though he did not know where he was going."

Hebrews 11:8 (NIV)

June 11

When faced with difficulty of any sort, embark upon a three-step process:

- Acknowledgement   *Do not run away from the problem.*
- Acceptance   *See the problem as an opportunity to grow*
- Adjustment   *Learn from it!*

_____

_____

_____

_____

_____

_____

_____

_____

"Consider it pure joy, my brothers, whenever you face trials of many kinds. Because you know that the testing of your faith develops perseverance. Perseverance must finish its work so that you may be mature and complete, not lacking anything."

James 1:2–4 (NIV)

June 12

Talent, in many ways, is much like a financial windfall. You have to manage it, making it grow and prosper. Certainly, it would be the height of foolishness to just sit on such a windfall, watching it stagnate and simply living off the interest, wouldn't it? Like untapped genius, nothing is more common than wasted talent. So, to succeed, you must engage in the proper investment of your talent.

_____

_____

_____

_____

_____

_____

_____

_____

_____

"Then he who had received the five talents went and traded with them and made another five talents. And likewise he who had received two, gained two more also. But he who had received one went and dug in the ground, and hid his Lord's money."

Matthew 25:16–18 (NIV)

June 13

To be a winner you have to think like one. Winners don't function the way most people do. They are always striving, always analyzing, and always questioning themselves. They tend to notice details that other people miss or overlook. Indeed, it is clear that great people have two things in common: a passion to succeed and an almost obsessive attention to detail.

_____

_____

_____

_____

_____

_____

_____

_____

_____

_____

"My son, preserve sound judgement and discernment, do not let them out of your sight."

Proverbs 3:21 (NIV)

June 14

A very old man woke up one morning and commenced planting the seeds of the mango tree in his garden. His neighbor came calling.

Neighbor: *"Old man, what are you doing?"*

Old man: *"I am planting mango trees."*

Neighbor: *Surely, you must know you can't possibly live long enough to eat mango from these trees. It takes years for them to grow."*

Old man: *"That maybe true, but others will. You see, all my life I have enjoyed mangoes planted by others. This is my own way of showing my gratitude."*

_____

_____

_____

"David thought, 'I will show kindness to Hanun, son of Nahash, just as his father showed kindness to me.'"

2 Samuel 10:2 (NIV)

June 15

Set your goals on short-, medium-, and long-term bases. What are your goals for the month? What are your goals for each quarter of the year? Overall, what are your goals for the year? What is your five-year strategic plan? Ten years from today, where will you be?

_____

_____

_____

_____

_____

_____

_____

_____

_____

_____

"During the seven years of abundance, the land produced plentifully. Joseph collected all the food produced in those seven years of abundance in Egypt, and stored it in the cities. ... There was famine in all the other lands but in the whole land of Egypt, there was food."

Genesis 41:47–48, 54 (NIV)

June 16

"When you do more than you are paid to do, eventually you will be paid more for what you do."

Zig Ziglar

This is quite true for two reasons:

First, if you do more than what you are paid to do, you will increase your value to your organization. In an effort not to lose you to a competitor, your superiors will promote you and pay you more. Secondly, you will increase your value to yourself, such that even if you had to leave your present organization, your improved skills will guarantee you even better pay at your next port of call.

_____

_____

_____

_____

_____

"Whatever you do, work at it with all your heart, as working for the Lord, not for men."

Colossians 3:23 (NIV)

June 17

When it comes to the commonplace activity of "saying something," I have come to the conclusion that there are two groups of people. Some people have something to say. Some others just have to say something. Refuse to engage in foolish talk and unnecessary arguments.

_____
_____
_____
_____
_____
_____
_____
_____
_____
_____
_____
_____

"Don't have anything to do with foolish and stupid arguments, because you know they produce quarrels."

2 Timothy 2:23 (NIV)

June 18

There is an interesting inverse relationship between you and life. When you are tough on yourself, life is going to be infinitely easier on you. Conversely, when you take things easy, life will become very tough for you. The path of self and spiritual development is a very long and arduous one, but it's a journey well worth taking.

"A sluggard does not plough in season, so at harvest time he looks but finds nothing."

Proverbs 20:4 (NIV)

June 19

Aim high. Elevate your sights. Mediocre ambitions seldom lead to great success since only big dreams can inspire big efforts. The world is a pyramid of struggling people. You must join in the struggle. You have no choice in the matter. But you can choose where to fight. Refuse to fight at the bottom of the pyramid. It's much too crowded down there. Rather, opt for the top. It's easier up there.

"If thou shalt hearken diligently unto the voice of the Lord thy God, to observe and to do all his commandments which I command thee this day, that the Lord thy God will set thee on high above all nations of the earth."

Deuteronomy 28:1 (KJV)

June 20

Giving and receiving may actually be two sides of the same coin. This is because inherent in the ability to give is the ability to receive, and this in turn is because anytime someone gives, another person receives, and anytime someone receives, another person has given. Thus, the cycle of flow of God's abundance in our lives continues unbroken. So, give without remembering, and receive without forgetting.

_____

_____

_____

_____

_____

_____

_____

_____

_____

"Remember this: Whoever sows sparingly will also reap sparingly, and whoever sows generously will also reap generously. Each man should give what he has decided in his heart to give, not reluctantly or under compulsion, for God loves a cheerful giver."

2 Corinthians 9:6–7 (NIV)

June 21

Adversity can break you, or it can make you. In many respects, adversity is very much like a knife. Grasp it by the handle and it will serve you well. Grasp it by the blade and it cuts you!

_____

_____

_____

_____

_____

_____

_____

_____

_____

_____

_____

"Not only so, but we also rejoice in our sufferings, because we know that suffering produces perseverance, perseverance, character; and character, hope. And hope does not disappoint."

Romans 5:3–5 (NIV)

June 22

A man was suffering from gradual amnesia (a gradual loss of memory).

Doctor: *"There's a brain operation we could do to restore your memory. However, it's delicate and a nerve might be severed causing total blindness. So, which would you rather have: your sight or your memory?"*

Patient: *"I'd rather have my sight. I'd rather see where I'm going than remember where I've been."*

Your past does not have to be your future. You can't forget your past, of course, but you don't have to live in it either. Forget your past mistakes. Forge ahead.

_____

_____

_____

"Forget the former things; do not dwell on the past."

Isaiah 43:18 (NIV)

June 23

Learn to choose your words carefully. They are the embodiment of great power. Absolutely refuse to denigrate yourself. Rather, confess the positive all the time. Rather than "Life is terrible," say, "Life is great. The good days are here, but the best is yet to come." Habitually turn your words into commands. When your mind becomes powerful enough, each command will become a royal decree and a self-fulfilling prophecy. For you, words and reality will have fused to become one.

"In the beginning was the Word, and the Word was with God, and the Word was God."

John 1:1 (NIV)

June 24

A young officer-cadet, due to a traffic hold-up, missed his flight back to the academy. His neighbors said, "How sad, now you will miss a whole day of lectures and military exercises." Thirty minutes after takeoff, the plane crashed into the lagoon, killing all his fellow cadet-officers, a whole generation of bright, young officers.

Do not grieve for what doesn't come, for what doesn't come may be to prevent disaster from coming.

_____

_____

_____

_____

_____

_____

_____

_____

_____

"Thou will keep him in perfect peace, whose mind is stayed on thee, because he trusteth in thee."

Isaiah 26:3 (KJV)

June 25

If you are internally dissatisfied with yourself, even if you had a whole country for your house, with all its people for your servants, all this will not be enough to make you content.

"I am not saying this because I am in need, for I have learned to be content whatever the circumstances."

Ecclesiastes 7:21 (KJV)

June 27

Worry is such an unfortunate habit, isn't it? Admittedly, real problems do exist, but often we expend so much energy on problems that do not exist, or worse still, we create new ones by dwelling on a myriad of bad things that might happen but never do. Resolve today to be so strong that nothing and nobody can disturb your peace of mind.

_____

_____

_____

_____

_____

_____

_____

_____

_____

_____

_____

_____

"Who of you by worrying can add a single hour to his life?"

Matthew 6:27 (NIV)

June 28

A man strolling on the sidewalk suddenly stopped, gripped his head in both hands, and screamed out to no one in particular, "Oh God, why me? Why? Why?" A passerby stopped, went over to him and tapped him on the shoulder, saying, "Hey, what do you mean, why you? So, who should it be? Me? My dad?"

Whenever you are faced with hardship, do not scream in anguish, rather turn trustfully to God.

_____

_____

_____

_____

_____

_____

_____

_____

_____

"God is our refuge and strength, an ever-present help in trouble."

Psalm 46:1 (NIV)

June 29

The greater a power anything has for good, the greater the power it also has for evil. After all, good swimmers drown, and good horse riders fall—both turn what they love into their misfortune.

_____
_____
_____
_____
_____
_____
_____
_____
_____
_____
_____
_____
_____
_____

"With the tongue we praise our Lord and Father, and with it we curse men, who have been made in God's likeness."

James 3:9 (NIV))

June 30

Young man:	*"Sir, I have a business idea, but everyone seems to think it won't work."*
Pastor:	*"Do you think it will work?"*
Young man:	*"Absolutely sir. I'm convinced I'm onto something big here."*
Pastor:	*"Well, to persevere in anything exceptional, especially in the face of discouragement, requires inner strength and the unshakeable conviction that you're right."*
Young man:	*"What should I do, pastor?"*
Pastor:	*"Care not for what others think. Act only in accordance with divine purpose. Do it!"*

"Then Peter and the other apostles answered and said, 'We ought to obey God rather than men.'"

Acts 5:29 (NIV)

July 1

The solving of a mathematical problem follows a process. So does the solving of a business or life problem. Define the problem clearly. What are all the possible causes of the problem? What are all the possible solutions? What is the best solution? What must this solution accomplish? Finally, delegate responsibility or take personal responsibility for its implementation.

"The heart of the discerning acquires knowledge, the ears of the wise seek it out."

Proverbs 18:15 (NIV)

July 2

We are all in the business of selling something or the other, and all advancement or profit comes from adding value of some kind. So, you will need to continually ask these questions:

- What can I do to increase my value to my customers?
- Better still, who are my ideal customers, and how do I attract more of them?
- Best of all, what would I have to do to deserve more of this type of customer?

Continually look for creative ways to add value by doing things faster, better, cheaper, and easier.

_____

_____

_____

_____

_____

"Do you see a man skilled in his work? He will serve before kings. He will not serve before obscure men."

Proverbs 22:29 (NIV)

July 3

Today, resolve to spice up your career. Go to your boss, tell him that you are determined to contribute maximally to the growth of the company so you want more responsibility. Once you get the extra assignment, complete it with speed and accuracy. Then, ask for even more!

_____
_____
_____
_____
_____
_____
_____
_____
_____
_____
_____
_____
_____

"And if ye have not been faithful in that which is another man's, who shall give you that which is your own?"

Luke 16:12 (KJV)

July 4

Your success will be in direct proportion to what you do after you do what you are expected to do. This is called going the extra mile. On this extra mile, there are usually no traffic jams! The reason? Few people travel this lonely stretch. It takes too much effort. So, you, the lone man on the extra mile, will be very conspicuous. Management will notice you. Your boss will notice you. It's you who will get recommended for that course. You will get that promotion. You will get that pay raise. You have suddenly become the golden boy. The sky is your limit!

"Now to him who is able to do immeasurably more than all we ask or imagine, according to his power that is at work within us, to him be the glory."

Ephesians 3:20 (NIV)

July 5

Your greatest challenge is the conquest of fear and the development of courage. Since anything you practice over and over eventually becomes a habit, you will develop courage by acting courageously anytime courage is called for. Remember: Courage is not the absence of fear. It is the mastery of fear. A courageous person goes forward in spite of fear.

"For God hath not given us the spirit of fear, but of power, and of love, and of a sound mind."

2 Timothy 1:7 (KJV)

July 6

He who teaches himself has a fool for a master.

_____
_____
_____
_____
_____
_____
_____
_____
_____
_____
_____
_____
_____
_____
_____

"You, then, who teach others, do you not teach yourself?"

Romans 2:21 (NIV)

July 7

Accusing others is not as good as accusing yourself. Demanding from others is not as good as demanding from yourself.

_____

_____

_____

_____

_____

_____

_____

_____

_____

_____

_____

_____

_____

_____

"Why do you look at the speck of sawdust in your brother's eye and pay no attention to the plank in your own eye?"

Matthew 7:3 (NIV)

July 8

What does it mean to concentrate on something? Real concentration is a sacrifice. This is because real concentration means sacrificing all other activities for a single goal, directing all thought, all emotion, all energy, and all force toward that single goal, possessing an ardent and passionate desire for the goal, and sustaining that desire for days, months, and even years. Consider how focused Jesus was on his mission.

_____

_____

_____

_____

_____

_____

_____

_____

_____

_____

"As the time approached for him to be taken up to heaven, Jesus resolutely set out for Jerusalem."

Luke 9:51 (NIV)

July 9

The very best qualities of strength, courage, character, and persistence are manifested in you when you face your challenges, great or small, squarely, responding positively and constructively.

"*Whoever can be trusted with very little can also be trusted with very much.*"

Luke 16:10 (NIV)

July 10

Yes, indeed, life is short. People start realizing this when they attain middle age. But it's not how long you live that counts, but how well you live. Making time count is more important, and much more profitable, than counting time.

"Show me, O Lord, my life's end and the number of my days; let me know how fleeting is my life. You have made my days a mere hand-breadth, the span of my years is as nothing before you. Each man's life is but a breath."

Psalm 39:4–5 (NIV)

July 11

At his seventy-fifth birthday, Mahatma Gandhi, the world-famous Indian nationalist leader, announced that he planned to live another fifty years. He revealed his blueprint for reaching the age of a century and a quarter, and it featured the following: An abundance of humor, a balanced diet, avoidance of all stimulants, adequate sleep, a deliberate refusal to be annoyed, angered, upset, or disturbed, an absolute resignation to the will of God, and prayers thrice daily. Gandhi, did not quite achieve his plan, as he died only three years later at the age of seventy eight. His prescription for longevity, however, has been proved to be quite valid, especially among the monks in Tibet.

_____

_____

_____

_____

_____

_____

_____

_____

"The prayer of a righteous man is powerful and effective."

James 5:16 (NIV)

July 12

One thing is clear: the fundamental requisite for a successful life is neither how much you know nor how hard you work (although of course, neither is to be trifled with). The most important factor is what you believe and how deep that belief is. You can do no more than you believe you can. You can be no more than you believe you are. Your belief pattern stimulates your power to achieve.

_____

_____

_____

_____

_____

_____

_____

_____

_____

_____

"Jesus said unto him, if thou canst believe, all things are possible to him that believeth."

Mark 9:23 (KJV)

July 13

Winners are different from most other people, and what makes them different is their self-confidence and determination. They see themselves differently from the way most people do. Knowing that they are the big children of a big God, they have developed a totally positive self-image.

"So do not throw away your confidence; it will be richly rewarded."

Hebrews 10:35 (NIV)

July 14

So, you have just lost your job. Refuse to be propelled into panic. Take a deep breath. Remain quiet, and listen. Rather than react to the situation, respond to it. Just like a solar eclipse, this too shall pass to reveal God's hidden motives. One door closes, and yet another opens—perhaps to an even bigger room. Simply wait on God.

"Wait on the Lord, be of good courage, and he shall strengthen thine heart; wait, I say, on the Lord."

Psalm 27:14 (KJV)

July 15

Henry Ford, the automobile maker, once said, "I am looking for a lot of men with an infinite capacity for not knowing what can't be done." In other words, he was looking for people with a possibility mentality. With this mentality, whatever idea your mind conceives, as long as your belief is total, brooking no doubt whatsoever, you can achieve it. So resolve today to be a "can do" and not a "can't do" person.

"If you can?" said Jesus. "Everything is possible for him who believes."

Mark 9:23 (NIV)

July 16

In any venture, there is no gain without some pain. After all, anyone who wants to be delivered from the pain of a bad tooth must be prepared to go through the agony of tooth extraction. You must be prepared to put in more to get more. You will have to invest effort into life for life to deliver its bounties to you. Decide today to despise the free lunch. Launch yourself into action. Start now!

"Do not be deceived. God cannot be mocked. A man reaps what he sows."

Galatians 6:7 (NIV)

July 17

Perhaps you are quite brilliant, sophisticated, and confident. Some people will surpass you in these qualities. On the other hand, you may not be particularly brilliant and perhaps you are even timid to the bargain. Some people would wish they were half as blessed as you are. Wherever you may belong between these two extremes, resolve today to start associating with those who are better than you. If, for instance, you are afflicted with self-doubt, avoid Brother Thomas (remember doubting Thomas?). Instead, visit and cultivate Father Abraham, the grand patriarch of the faith family.

"Whatever you have learned or received or heard from me—put it into practice."

Philippians 4:9 (NIV)

July 18

A good leader is one who knows the way. He also shows the way. But best of all, he also goes the way. This is why, as a leader, people will more readily follow you if you roll up your sleeves and set the pace, rather than issue orders from an armchair.

_____

_____

_____

_____

_____

_____

_____

_____

_____

_____

_____

_____

"Shepherd the flock of God which is among you ... not as being lords over those entrusted to you, but being examples to the flock."

1 Peter 5:2–3 (KJV)

July 19

"*You can count the number of seeds in an apple but you cannot count the number of apples from a seed.*"

Dr. Robert Schuller

It is only as you give the seed away to the soil can you expect to receive the harvest. In due time, too.

What seed have you sown today?

_____

_____

_____

_____

_____

_____

_____

_____

"*And let us not be weary in well doing, for in due season we shall reap, if we faint not.*"

Galatians 6:9 (KJV)

July 20

"A journey of one thousand miles begins with the first step."

Ancient Chinese Proverb

How true this is! For nothing can be accomplished without that first step. One fact is incontrovertible: If you refuse to start, then most certainly, you will not arrive.

_____

_____

_____

_____

_____

_____

_____

_____

_____

_____

"And the Lord said unto me, behold, I have begun to give Sihon and his land before thee, begin to possess, that thou may inherit his land."

Deuteronomy 2:31 (KJV)

July 21

Wisdom is much more than knowledge, much of which you can gain on your own. Rather, it is the ability to apply that knowledge to everyday life. It is a treasure you must seek with all your heart.

"And if you look for it as for silver and search for it as for hidden treasure. Then you will understand the fear of the Lord and find the knowledge of God. For the Lord gives wisdom."

Proverbs 2:4–6 (NIV)

July 22

Consider this: How can you even attempt to climb up the ladder of success clad in the costume of failure? If you do not see yourself as a winner, how can you possibly perform as a winner? Today, take off the costume of failure and start to climb the ladder of success, because you are a winner. Winners have God on their side.

_____
_____
_____
_____
_____
_____
_____
_____
_____
_____
_____
_____

"If God is for us, who can be against us?"

Romans 8:31 (NIV)

July 23

Anyone who would be a top performer ought to have a small room in his home, separate from his study, where the only furniture is a chair and a small table, on which should always be a clean sheet of paper and a pen. So, withdraw from the crowd and practice thinking on paper. An extraordinary thing seems to happen between the brain and the hand when you write. You think better. Your perception is sharper. You are smarter.

"He withdrew about a stone's throw beyond them, knelt down and prayed."

Luke 22:41 (NIV)

July 24

Permit me to suggest four guidelines that will assist you in drawing up your own personal strategic plan:

- *Where am I now?*
- *Where would I like to be in the future?*
- *How did I get to where I am today?*
- *What do I do now, to get from where I am to where I'd like to be?*

This is strategic thinking. As our God is a strategic planner, so must we be.

_____

_____

_____

_____

_____

_____

_____

"Come now, and let us reason together, saith the Lord."

Isaiah 1:18 (KJV)

July 25

No man is so poor as him whose only wealth is money.

This is absolutely true because, while the world measures success by the size of a man's bank account, God measures the man's success by the size of his heart.

_____
_____
_____
_____
_____
_____
_____
_____
_____
_____
_____
_____
_____

"For a man's life consisteth not in the abundance of the things which he possesseth."

Luke 12:15 (KJV)

July 26

I recall, once, in Lagos, Nigeria, being trapped in one of those notorious and seemingly interminable traffic hold-ups. I glanced at the car next to mine only to be presented with the most fascinating spectacle. The driver had somehow worked himself up into self-righteous anger. He plonked down on his horn incessantly, angrily wiped the profuse sweat off his brow and muttered under his breath. He was a study in infantile impatience.

When you become a patient man, you will react not merely with feelings, but with intelligence. Refusing to respond with uncontrolled emotion, your motivation will be on a spiritual basis, allowing you to develop philosophical and patient control. That way, you will not become easily frustrated and upset.

Indeed, patience is a great word. It implies maturity and spiritual sophistication.

_____

_____

_____

"In your patience, possess ye your souls."

Luke 21:19 (KJV)

July 27

Strive strenuously for knowledge, and then share it with others. Share it through words of course, but more importantly through deeds. Set an example. That is the best way of committing what you have learned to faithful men and women, who, in turn, can teach others.

_____
_____
_____
_____
_____
_____
_____
_____
_____
_____
_____
_____

"And the things that thou hast heard of me among many witnesses, the same commit thou to faithful men, who shall be able to teach others also."

2 Timothy 2:2 (KJV)

July 28

I am shortsighted, so I wear glasses. The lenses help my eyes focus crisply and clearly. That is how your life will become clear and focused when you have mastered your mission. You will then see where you are going and act in faith to get there. For you, the journey and the destination will then become equally pleasurable.

_____
_____
_____
_____
_____
_____
_____
_____
_____
_____

"I hold fast to your statutes, O Lord ... I run in the path of your commands."

Psalm 119:31-32 (NIV)

July 29

"It is the nature of every man to err, but only a fool perseveres in error."

Cicero (106–43BC)
Roman Orator and Statesman

Unless you agree to learn from life, how will you stop making the same mistakes and struggling with the same problems over and over again?

The truth is really quite simple: If you learn from a defeat you haven't really lost!

"As a dog returns to its vomit, so a fool repeats his folly."

Proverbs 26:11 (NIV)

July 30

The greatest secret of sustainable financial success is dual in nature. Whenever any money accrues to you, do two things immediately:

1. Pay 10% of your gross earnings to God as tithe.
2. Pay 10% to yourself.

It is after these payments that you will pay your bills. The 10% you paid yourself is investible funds. It is not to be saved for the rainy day. You must allow such monies to grow through wise investments. After all, if you chose to kill your children, can you possibly have grand-children?

"Bring the whole tithe into the storehouse, that there may be food in my house. Test me in this, says the Lord Almighty, and see if I will not throw open the floodgates of heaven and pour out so much blessing that you will not have room enough for it."

Malachi 3:10 (NIV)

July 31

"If you want to fly with the eagles, you cannot continue to scratch the sand with the turkeys."

Zig Ziglar

How very true! To achieve greatness you must aspire to greatness. To achieve excellence, you must set excellent standards and commit to achieving them. After all, God, who saw fit to create us in His own image, is the highest standard of excellence.

"O Lord our Lord, how excellent is thy name in all earth! Who has set thy glory above the heavens."

Psalm 8:1 (KJV)

August 1

Successful people are always goal-oriented because goal setting is the first step in turning the invisible into the visible. It is the foundation of all success. Like all other activities, it demands an articulate process. To this end, over the next few days, I shall present a nine-step goal setting and achieving process which, if given the seriousness it deserves, will turn your life around. For today however, affirm to yourself: "Goal setting is my master skill of success."

"I press on towards the goal."

Philippians 3:14 (NIV)

August 2

So you have a goal. Write it down in explicit detail. This turns your goal from a mere wish to an articulated desire. Is it your personal home? Where will it be located? How many rooms will it have? Visualize it. What does it look like at the front and at the back? What is its color?

Now set a deadline. When will you move into this house?

_____

_____

_____

_____

_____

_____

_____

_____

_____

_____

"I intend, therefore, to build a temple for the Name of the Lord my God."

1 Kings 5:5 (KJV)

August 3

List out all the reasons why you want to achieve your goal. These are the benefits and rewards that will accrue to you as you accomplish the goal. They are your motivating factors. The more you continually think of them, the more likely it is that you will put in the effort necessary to achieve your goal.

"Remember me for this, O my God, and do not blot out what I have so faithfully done for the house of my God and its services."

Nehemiah 13:14 (NIV)

August 4

Clearly identify your starting position. If you have absolute clarity about where you are coming from and where you are going, the more likely it is that you will end up where you want to be. So, where are you now?

"Naomi and her daughters-in-law prepared to return home from there. With her two daughters-in-law, she left the place where she had been living and set out on the road."

Ruth 1:6–7(NIV)

August 5

List out all the possible obstacles that stand between you and your goal. What is the biggest single obstacle? What can you do to surmount this "rock of Gibraltar"? But remember, whatever this obstacle is, refuse to dwell on its size. Rather, dwell on the power of God.

"The Lord who delivered me from the paw of the lion and the paw of the bear will deliver me from the hand of this Philistine."

1 Samuel 17:37 (NIV)

August 6

You must learn what you need to know to accomplish what you want to accomplish. What additional information do you require to achieve your goal? If you don't have the information yourself, is it a skill or knowledge that you can acquire through study and/or practice? Can you engage someone else, a consultant perhaps, with this knowledge? Who else has achieved success in this area who could possibly avail you of useful advice?

_____
_____
_____
_____
_____
_____
_____
_____
_____

"If the axe is dull, and its edge unsharpened, more strength is needed but skill will bring success."

Ecclesiastes 10:10 (NIV)

August 7

Make a list of all the people whose help and cooperation you will need to achieve your goal. Note two facts: One, others will help you achieve your goal if they feel that they will be compensated in some way. Two, people will help you achieve your goal if you are willing to help them achieve theirs. For these two reasons, you must build up a reservoir of goodwill by always doing more than expected of you and then taking every opportunity to help others. To create the quality and quantity of your returns, you must increase the quality and quantity of your services.

"Serve wholeheartedly, as if you were serving the Lord, not men."

Ephesians 6:7 (NIV)

August 8

Draw up your master plan for success today. Simply ask yourself seven questions, and answer them:

- *What do I want?*
- *When do I want it?*
- *Why do I want it?*
- *Where am I starting from?*
- *What obstacles must I overcome?*
- *What information will I require?*
- *Who are those people whose help I will need?*

_____

_____

_____

_____

_____

_____

_____

"For which of you, intending to build a tower, sitteth not down first, and counteth the cost, whether he have sufficient to finish it?"

Luke 14:28 (KJV)

August 9

Today, play a mental game. Play around with mental pictures. Create a clear and vivid picture of your goal as it would appear if it were already achieved. Now, imagine your mind as some form of screen. Replay this picture over and over again on this screen. What you see is what you get!

_____

_____

_____

_____

_____

_____

_____

_____

_____

_____

_____

"And the Lord answered me, and said, write the vision, and make it plain upon tables."

Habakkuk 2:2 (NIV)

August 10

Make a decision up-front that you will never give up, and back up your goal and plan with persistence and tenacious determination. Simply refuse to consider the possibility of failure. Nothing succeeds like success. Develop the success habit by doing something each day to move you towards the realization of your goal. Review your goal every morning, think of it during the day, and review it again at bedtime. After ensuring that your goal is in accord with God's will for you, make it your magnificent obsession!

"You need to persevere so that when you have done the will of God, you will receive what He has promised."

Hebrew 10:36 (NIV)

August 11

Resolve today to become a member of the top 10% club. Let us play with figures. You can beat 50% of the people by working hard and smart. You can beat a further 40% by living right. This means you can put yourself in the top 10% bracket by working hard and smart, and by living right. You work smart by being an original and by having a strategy. You live right by subscribing to integrity, and being at peace with God and with man. See you at the top.

_____

_____

_____

_____

_____

_____

_____

_____

_____

_____

_____

"Not slothful in business, fervent in spirit, serving the Lord."

Romans 12:11 (KJV)

August 12

You cannot promote your boss. Neither can you give him a bonus. But you can reward him by doing any or all of these:

- Praise him privately or publicly.
- Support his goals privately or publicly.
- Relieve him of some routine jobs so that he can take the afternoon off.
- Help him train new employees.
- Most importantly, let him know how proud you are to be working with him.

_____

_____

_____

_____

_____

_____

_____

"Whoso keepeth the fig tree shall eat the fruit thereof, so he that waiteth on his master shall be honoured."

Proverbs 27:18 (KJV)

August 13

Quite often, it would seem that a desperate feeling of hopelessness is the first step on the path of spiritual awakening. In fact, many people do not awaken to the awesome reality of God and the experience of genuine transformation until they go through the experience of despair, despondence, and abject emptiness.

_____

_____

_____

_____

_____

_____

_____

_____

_____

_____

_____

_____

_____

_____

"Surely it was for my benefit that I suffered such anguish."

Isaiah 38:17 (NIV)

August 14

It is rightly said that if all the malignant gossip in the world were to be halted for just a second, an eerie quiet and silence would envelop the world. Refuse to join in the gossip tendency.

As a step toward this, affirm to yourself today:

"I will speak no ill of anyone. Certainly, I will say nothing of anyone that I cannot repeat in his or her presence. I declare that if I have nothing charitable or neutral to say about someone, I shall remain silent."

"Set a guard over my mouth, O Lord; keep watch over the door of my mouth."

Psalm 141:3 (NIV)

August 15

"I have learned to find out the better side of human nature, and to enter men's hearts. Without realizing it, I had found the secret of success. I began to look on every difficulty as an opportunity for service; a challenge which could draw out of me greater resources of intelligence and imagination."

Mahatma Gandhi

_____

_____

_____

_____

_____

_____

_____

_____

_____

_____

"For our light and momentary troubles are achieving for us an eternal glory that far outweighs them all."

2 Corinthians 4:17 (NIV)

August 16

"Seek first to understand, then to be understood."

Stephen Covey
The 7 Habits of Highly Effective People

This is the bedrock, or foundation if you will, of empathic communication. Almost always, when a person is speaking to you, most of the message or information he or she intends to convey to you is actually left unsaid, or at best is couched in convoluted language. In active listening, it becomes your job to unearth those things that have been left unsaid. That way you understand each other better. You engage in active listening by asking relevant, thoughtful questions. That way, you listen with your ears and with your mouth. This is active listening.

_____

_____

_____

_____

_____

"He who answers before listening—that is his folly and his shame."

Proverbs 18:13 (NIV)

August 17

Nothing is gained by making yourself small and insignificant other than to manifest smallness and insignificance in your life.

_____
_____
_____
_____
_____
_____
_____
_____
_____
_____
_____
_____
_____
_____

"Jesus answered them, Is it not written in your law, I have said you are gods?"

John 10:34 (NIV)

August 18

True love is actually an action and not just a feeling. Since we cannot command feelings but can command an active determination of our will, it therefore follows that we can, by a conscious act of will, choose to love one another. Put quite simply, even when we don't feel love for someone, if we chose to show love, the corresponding feeling will usually follow. This is unconditional love.

_____

_____

_____

_____

_____

_____

_____

_____

_____

"Love is patient, love is kind. It does not envy, it does not boast, it is not proud; It is not rude, it is not self-seeking, it is not easily angered, it keeps no record of wrongs."

1 Corinthians 13:4, 5 (NIV)

August 19

A man in America embarked upon a thirteen-year long "speech strike" to bring attention to issues of environmental degradation and pollution. It worked! Media pressure eventually provoked the authorities to institute necessary reforms. On a personal note, however, his long silence taught him what it meant to really listen to others. Talking less can both help us to hear more and be heard more. Indeed, silence can be golden, and is often much more eloquent than words.

"Even a fool is thought wise if he keeps silent, and discerning if he holds his tongue."

Proverbs 17:28 (NIV)

August 20

"He who has conquered the world is great. But he who has conquered himself is greater still."

LaoTze
Chinese General

You conquer yourself when you have "tamed" yourself into a state of self-discipline. Self-discipline simply means doing what needs to be done, when it needs to be done, whether it's convenient or not. This prayer will help you:

"Help me, Lord, to exercise necessary self-discipline in my life that I may be a daily overcomer."

_____

_____

_____

_____

_____

_____

"Create in me a pure heart, O God, and renew a steadfast spirit within me."

Psalm 51:10 (NIV)

August 21

The people of Delphi in Greece have a saying:

"Know thyself."

Polonius's last piece of advice to his son, Laertes, in Shakespeare's Hamlet was: "To thine own self be true." Yes, indeed, self-knowledge is the greatest source of personal power. Careful self-examination and a sincere willingness to engage in consistent self-improvement provide the foundation for right living.

_____

_____

_____

_____

_____

_____

_____

_____

"And ye shall know the truth, and the truth shall make you free."

John 8:32 (KJV)

August 22

If there is righteousness in man's heart, he will have character.

If he has character, there will be harmony in his home.

If there is harmony in his home, the nation will be orderly.

If there is order in the nation, the world will know peace.

_____

_____

_____

_____

_____

_____

_____

_____

_____

_____

_____

"Sow for yourselves righteousness, reap the fruit of unfailing love ...
Until He comes and showers righteousness upon you."

Hosea 10:12 (NIV)

August 23

Our minds are usually filled with a random, all-day chatter, which is actually just a mindless, inner monologue consisting of an amazing mass of jumbled, distracting thoughts, ranging from the sublime to the ridiculous. Clearing your "inner self" of this random chatter and living in what I call "God-centered, present-moment awareness" will leave your mind fertile for the sowing of creative seeds. That way, what you desire and what desires you can grow. My own practice is to repeat this statement continually throughout the day:

"God is the only presence and power in my person."

This way, you carry God's presence with you all day long and turn your very existence itself into a prayer.

_____

_____

_____

_____

_____

"Pray continually."

1 Thessalonians 15:17 (**NIV**)

August 24

It is always seemingly humiliating to be reduced in rank, privileges or responsibility. But perhaps we ought to substitute the word "humbling" for humiliating. This is because it would perhaps be more appropriate to view such occurrences as things we have to experience as part of God's training in our lives. Humility is not a sign of weakness but evidence of power and character. Ask for the grace to do the humble task with a joyful spirit.

"Humble yourselves, therefore, under God's mighty hand, that he may lift you up in due time."

1 Peter 5:6 (NIV)

August 25

Fifty-five-year-old Dele Charles sits atop the DC Group, a holding company that is involved in hotels, shipping, insurance, car dealership, construction, telecommunications, and aircraft charter services. But he is a most unusual tycoon. He goes by the title "vice chairman of the DC Group," although he is indisputably the founder and sole owner of the conglomerate. To date, the identity of the chairman of the group remains obscure. But not to me. I was privileged to make a presentation to the full house of board members of the group. To my utter amazement, the high-backed swivel chair at the head of the table remained empty throughout, with the name plaque in front of it reading: "God—Chairman"!

"But Gideon told them: I will not rule over you, nor will my son rule over you. The Lord will rule over you."

1 Judges 8:23 (NIV)

August 26

The highly fortified doors to a bank vault usually possess a combination lock, and almost always, it's only the bank manager, and perhaps another official, who have the clue to opening the lock. In many respects, life is like a combination lock. With the right numbers in the right sequence, you can open up life and live as joyfully as you desire.

"I have come that they may have life, and have it to the full."

John 10:10

August 27

One fact about material acquisition is incontrovertible. God showers His material blessings on us for our enjoyment. However, there can be no iota of sustainable security in wealth. This means that it would be wrong for us to place our confidence in our possessions. Indeed, this would be misplaced confidence. Rather, our confidence should be in the giver, and not the gift. In other words, worship the giver, and not the gift.

_____

_____

_____

_____

_____

_____

_____

_____

_____

"Command those who are rich in this world not to be arrogant nor to put their hope in wealth, which is so uncertain, but to put their hope in God, who richly provides us with everything for our enjoyment."

1 Timothy 6:17 (NIV)

August 28

"If people only knew the medicinal value of good cheer and laughter, most physicians would be out of business."

Sydney Bremer

Commit to cultivating excellent interpersonal relationship skills. These skills will contribute fully 85% to your success. Always wear a cheerful smile. Be willing to lend a helping hand. Express your gratitude for those little favors. Be willing to forgive effortlessly. Be willing to say "I'm sorry" if need be. Police your temper. And once again, if only to underscore its importance, always wear a cheerful smile!

_____

_____

_____

_____

_____

_____

_____

_____

_____

"A happy heart makes the face cheerful, but heartache crushes the spirit."

Proverbs 15:13 (NIV)

August 29

It was noon already and the young man was still asleep. His mother shook him angrily to waken him. Rousing from sleep with enormous effort and great reluctance, he rubbed his eyes drowsily and said, "Oh mum, you have just interrupted a great dream. I dreamed that I owned a condominium in Florida, a townhouse in Park lane in London and a mansionette on Lekki."

Mum: *"It still remains a dream, doesn't it?"*

Son: *"Yes mum, but I claim them all."*

Mum: *"Whether you can validly claim them or not is immaterial. What is important is that you wake up."*

His mother was right. The best way to make your dreams come true is to wake up.

"He who sleeps during harvest is a disgraceful son."

Proverbs 10:5 (NIV)

August 30

A young boy had behaved very badly, and his grandfather, an elderly, wise pastor, attempted to counsel him.

Pastor: "It's as if we have two lions inside of us. One is good, the other is bad, and they both demand our obedience to them."

Boy: "Which one wins?"

Pastor: "The one we feed!"

When an evil desire demands to be fed, we must say no! Always remember that what you feed will ultimately control you.

_____

_____

_____

_____

"Clothe yourselves with the Lord Jesus Christ, and do not think about how to gratify the desires of the sinful nature."

Romans 13:14 (NIV)

August 31

What you get by attaining your goals is not quite as important as what you become by reaching them. This implies that attaining the goal is not all that matters. What quality of life did you experience along the way? Your answer to this question is important because one great dividend that comes out of the struggle to achieve is strength of character.

"And the God of all grace, who called you to his eternal glory in Christ, after you have suffered a little while, will himself restore you and make you strong, firm and steadfast."

1 Peter 5:10 (NIV)

September 1

On awakening, the gazelle knows it must run faster than the fastest lion or be killed and eaten for breakfast. Conversely, the lion knows it must outrun the slowest gazelle or starve to death. Whether you are a lion or a gazelle, at sunrise, you had better be running.

If you are not seeking God, the devil is seeking you. Therefore, refuse to enter the day complacently. For you, it's spiritual warfare every day.

_____

_____

_____

_____

_____

_____

_____

_____

_____

"Be self-controlled and alert. Your enemy the devil prowls around like a roaring lion looking for someone to devour."

1 Peter 5:8 (NIV)

September 2

"Favour is the cure for man's emptiness."

Bishop David O. Oyedepo

Therefore, affirm to yourself always: "As favor reaches me, emptiness leaves me."

"And I will give this people favour in the sight of the Egyptians; and it shall come to pass, that, when ye go, ye shall not go empty."

Exodus 3:21 (KJV)

September 3

Still on favor. It would seem as if favor has its own mystery. It is God's reward system for those who have been dedicated and committed to Him. Significantly also, we all have the right to favor, but do not all have access to it. So, today, pray for favor, like Jabez did 3,000 years ago.

"*Jabez called out to the God of Israel, Oh, that you would bless me and enlarge my territory! Let your hand be with me, and keep me from harm so that I will be free from pain. And God granted his request.*"

1 Chronicles 4:10 (NIV)

September 4

Consider this. Money will buy a bed, but not sleep. It will buy food, but not appetite. It will buy amusement, but not happiness. It will buy a house, but not a home. Whether you have plenty or a little of money, always remember that it's not really a part of you. While money is representative of God's abundance and is not evil, you must not be dominated by it. Remember also what Paul said, "Godliness with contentment is great gain."

"But godliness with contentment is great gain. For we brought nothing into the world, and we can take nothing out of it."

1 Timothy 6:6–7 (NIV)

September 5

Still on money. All the money you will ever need to fulfill your obligations has been kept somewhere for you. It is in the pockets of the people around you. However, they will release this money to you only if you add value of some kind to their lives. You can do this by offering some service or selling some product. Since you now know where your money is kept, resolve today to discover what product you should sell or what service you should offer to access these funds of theirs. But remember, all you do must be in accordance with God's principles.

"With me are riches and honour, enduring wealth and prosperity."

Proverbs 8:18 (NIV)

September 6

"Each delay is perfectly fine, for we are within the safe hands of God."

Madame Guyon (1648–1717)

For most of us, waiting can be very traumatic. Delays make us anxious, impatient and annoyed. God's delay baffles us, and we ask, "For how long, my God?" But remember, God never says "wait awhile" unless He's planning some intervention. Faith never gives up. Those delays are used by God to give us humility, serenity, strength and patience. Wait patiently for Him.

"For the revelation awaits an appointed time, it speaks of the end and will not prove false. Though it linger, wait for it; it will certainly come and not delay."

Habbakuk 2:3 (NIV)

September 7

Two gossips were chatting. One said to the other, "I'm afraid I can't tell you anymore about Mary. I've already told you more than I heard." Before you share information that could possibly be considered gossip, ask yourself three questions:

- *Is it the truth?*
- *Even if it's the truth, do I really need to share it?*
- *Is it kind?*

Stop gossip in its tracks.

_____

_____

_____

_____

_____

_____

_____

_____

"A gossip betrays a confidence, but a trustworthy man keeps a secret."

Proverbs 11:13 (NIV)

September 8

"A winner is big enough to admit his mistakes, smart enough to profit from them and strong enough to correct them."

John Maxwell

Admitting the mistake is a start.

Correcting it is a step forward.

Following through guarantees success.

All these require humility, one of the hallmarks of a winner.

_____

_____

_____

_____

_____

_____

_____

"Humility and the fear of the Lord bring wealth and honour and life."

Proverbs 22:4 (NIV)

September 9

If it is worth doing at all, it is worth doing well. If it is worth doing well, then it is worth doing poorly at first. Refuse to give up. The common refrain that "practice makes perfect" may not be entirely accurate.

Actually, it would seem that it is imperfect practice that eventually makes perfect.

_____

_____

_____

_____

_____

_____

_____

_____

_____

_____

"But when perfection comes, the imperfect disappears."

1 Corinthians 13:10 (NIV)

September 10

Today, contemplate in some depth about prayer. Think about the enormous power inherent in prayer. To me, it would seem that genuine and authentic prayer is to invite divine desire to express itself through us. It should be a petition for what is for our highest purpose and good and for the greater benefit of mankind. Shouldn't the resultant unity with the Divine translate to a communion with God in which we ask for strength and the inner awareness to handle whatever confronts us?

_____
_____
_____
_____
_____
_____
_____
_____
_____

"He kneeled upon his knees three times a day and prayed and gave thanks before his God, as he did afore time."

Daniel 6:10 (NIV)

September 11

One of the greatest habits you can develop is that of maintaining silence, so as to actively listen to another person. To inculcate this habit, you must practice four things:

- *A suppression of your ego.*
- *Doing away with the need to justify your actions.*
- *Total and unconditional acceptance of the other person.*
- *A willingness and the humility to learn from each and every situation.*

"If only you would be altogether silent, for you that would be wisdom."

Job 13:5 (NIV)

September 12

What seems to you a terrible ordeal is often the quickest way, sometimes the only way, in the time God has allotted you, to help you evolve to refine your character until it becomes what it's supposed to be: an immortal diamond shining like the light of a thousand suns.

"Dear friends, do not be surprised at the painful trial you are suffering, as though something strange were happening to you."

1 Peter 4:12 (NIV)

September 13

Anytime you experience a failure, ask yourself ten questions: Why did I fail? What lessons have I learnt? Am I grateful for the experience? How can I turn the failure into success? Where do I go from here? Who else has failed in this way and how can he help me? How can my experience help others from failing? Did I fail because of another person, my situation, or myself? Did I actually fail or did I fall short of unrealistically high standards? In the circumstances, where did I succeed as well as fail?

_____

_____

_____

_____

_____

_____

_____

_____

_____

"It is the glory of God to conceal a matter, to search out a matter is the glory of kings."

Proverbs 25:2 (NIV)

September 14

I have studied, in some detail, the lives of great men and women. It seems when they are inspired to take on an extraordinary project, great purpose is born in them. Their thoughts break free of any shackles, their minds transcend limitations and their consciousness expands in all directions. Their dormant forces, powers of faculty, and talents all come alive, and they become the very epitome of God's energy and creativity. Pray that you may have the grace of such vibrancy in your life.

_____

_____

_____

_____

_____

_____

_____

_____

_____

"Whatever your hand finds to do, do it with all your might."

Ecclesiastes 9:10 (NIV)

September 15

Millionaire: *"Others may need prayer, but I don't. I worked hard for all I have. I didn't ask God for anything. I'm a self-made man."*

Passerby: *"Sir, there's one thing lacking in your life that you might just consider praying for."*

Millionaire: *"Oh? And what might that be?"*

Passerby: *"A small dose of humility, sir."*

Indeed the greatest danger of worldly success is self-sufficiency. It so easily masks spiritual poverty. When we are filled with pride, we leave no space for wisdom, for, strictly speaking, there is no such thing as a self-made person.

"You say, I am rich, I have acquired wealth and do not need a thing. But you do not realise that you are wretched, pitiful, poor, blind, and naked."

Revelations 3:17 (NIV)

September 16

I once had cause to visit with a gentleman who was at the peak of legislative leadership in my country, Nigeria. As he saw me off to my car, I inadvertently stepped into a puddle of stagnant rain water. He ordered me to take off my shoe, and, producing a clean cloth, and against my protestations, personally wiped the shoe clean of all trace of mud. I was dumbfounded! The man was a study in humility. These were his parting words to me. "We have to be humble to anyone we meet. If I place myself above others, their wisdom cannot flow up to me. But if I place myself below them, their wisdom can flow down to me, as if propelled by some form of spiritual gravity."

_____

_____

_____

_____

_____

_____

"For everyone who exalts himself will be humbled and he who humbles himself will be exalted."

Luke 8:14 (NIV)

September 17

The little seed started to sprout. It said to itself, "What flower shall I become?

"I don't want to be a rose. It has thorns.

"I wouldn't want to be a lily. It's too dull.

"I definitely don't want to be a violet. It's too small."

On and on it went, criticizing each flower type. Finally, this little fault-finding seed woke up one morning and found itself an ordinary weed!

_____

_____

_____

_____

"Do not think of yourself more highly than you ought, but rather think of yourself with sober judgement, in accordance with the measure of faith God has given you."

Romans 12:3 (NIV)

September 18

Today, say this prayer of humility:

"Lord, remind me constantly that I have nothing except what you give me, and can do nothing except what you enable me to do."

"A man can receive only what is given him from heaven."

John 3:27 (NIV)

September 19

Self-control is strength, right thought is mastery, and because power lies at the heart of tranquility, calmness, itself, is power.

Today, find time to sit quietly and affirm to yourself:

"Calm and quiet is my soul before God."

_____

_____

_____

_____

_____

_____

_____

_____

_____

_____

_____

"Quiet! Be still!"

Mark 4:39 (NIV)

September 20

You are where your attention takes you. In fact, you are your attention. If your attention is scattered, you are scattered. If your attention is focused, you are focused. When your attention is in the past, you are in the past. When your attention is in the present moment, you are in the presence of God, and God is present in you.

Little wonder, therefore, that a wise man once told mind-body medicine expert, Deepak Chopra, "The past is history, the future a mystery, but this moment is a gift. That is why this moment is called the present."

"Be still, and know that I am God."

Psalm 46:10 (NIV)

September 21

A friend's car has an interesting feature. Whenever a stranger touches it, an alarm goes off in the form of a shrill, persistent noise. Quite good as a security measure. Call it a warning whistle. Our conscience can work like that. When it gives you a warning whistle, pay attention! Your conscience is a guiding light, telling you wrong from right. Be thankful if you have a good one because it is one of the best friends you'll ever have. Insist on maintaining a clear conscience.

"Hold onto faith and a good conscience. Some have rejected these and so have shipwrecked their faith."

1 Timothy 1:19 (NIV)

September 22

"When you give thanks to God for His finger, He will show you His hand."

Bishop David O. Oyedepo

"It is good to praise the Lord and make music to your name, O most high."

Psalm 92:1 (NIV)

September 23

To really succeed, you need real faith, which is simply an inner vision of great spiritual laws. This faith allows you to see what you desire even before attaining it, much like the farmer who holds seeds in his hands and sees the stalks of corn that fill his fields at harvest time. All great men and women have this type of faith.

_____

_____

_____

_____

_____

_____

_____

_____

_____

_____

_____

_____

"Now faith is being sure of what we hope for and certain of what we do not see."

Hebrew 11:1 (NIV)

September 24

Very successful people develop that rare ability to be totally present, existing only in the present moment. They tend to become completely absorbed in the moment. This is because they know that it is only in the present moment that action has real meaning. They do not think too much about the future either, since they know that their actions in the present will determine the outcome of their future.

_____
_____
_____
_____
_____
_____
_____
_____
_____
_____
_____
_____

"Deep calls to deep."

Psalm 42:7 (NIV)

September 25

You are what and where you are because you have first imagined it, wittingly or unwittingly. The truth is that all things are created twice—first in the spiritual realm, and then later in the physical realm. This is the reason why the creative visualization of what you desire, backed by a fervent and humble petition to God, is one of the most powerful spiritual exercises you will ever embark upon.

_____

_____

_____

_____

_____

_____

_____

_____

_____

"And if we know that he hears us—whatever we ask—we know that we have what we asked of him."

1 John 5:15 (NIV)

September 26

Today, I humbly crave your indulgence to give me your sincere answer to an amazingly simple question:

"What have you always wanted to do but have been afraid to attempt?"

Now, confront your fears headlong, and prepare to do that thing!

_____

_____

_____

_____

_____

_____

_____

_____

_____

"Have I not commanded you? Be strong and courageous. Do not be terrified; do not be discouraged, for the Lord your God will be with you wherever you go."

Joshua 1:9 (NIV)

September 27

If you talk when you are angry, you will make the best speech you will always regret. Nothing is opened by mistake more often than the mouth. There is a time to speak and a time to be silent.

_____
_____
_____
_____
_____
_____
_____
_____
_____
_____
_____
_____
_____

"Everyone should be quick to listen, slow to speak and slow to become angry."

James 1:19 (NIV)

September 28

A life that is not subjected to heartbreaking adversity is rare indeed. Job said it all: "Man who is born of woman is of few days and full of trouble." How true! However, in dealing victoriously with our personal and painful experiences, what we need is the ability to endure without emotional collapse or spiritual bitterness. This is why it is often during great trial that great faith is born.

_____

_____

_____

_____

_____

_____

_____

_____

_____

_____

_____

"Naked I came from my mother's womb, and naked I shall depart. The Lord gave and the Lord has taken away."

Job 1:21 (NIV)

September 29

"Every day is God's day. But the day you get it right is your own day. Today, you will get it right in Jesus name."

Bishop David O. Oyedepo

"This is the day the Lord has made; let us rejoice and be glad in it."

Psalm 118:24 (NIV)

September 30

Extraordinary people are concentrated, firmly grounded in the center of their being. Once they receive God's command, they swing into action, and nothing can distract them, since they know that real concentration is a sacrifice. They pursue their goal to the exclusion of all irrelevant activities, becoming almost childlike in their total absorption in the task at hand. Dissolving into this love of the present moment, their victory is all the more remarkable, since whatever we do with love is invariably crowned with success.

_____

_____

_____

_____

_____

_____

_____

_____

"No-one who puts his hand to the plough and looks back is fit for service in the kingdom of God."

Luke 9:62 (NIV)

October 1

Today is celebrated as Independence Day in my country, Nigeria. The independence of a nation necessarily connotes a state of complete sovereignty, in which actual or self-styled colonialists leave a country to fend for itself, devoid of administrative or other interference. Put in terms that may sound perhaps infantile, a country is now left to think for itself.

To succeed, you must learn to think for yourself. This is because the quest for excellence demands that you look beyond appearances. You cannot afford to be content with the superficial.

"Righteousness exalts a nation."

Proverbs 14:34 (NIV)

October 2

God's presence is felt only where He is celebrated, and not where He is tolerated. This is why the declaration of your testimony is so important. Your testimony serves to further release God's awesome power in your life. The more you celebrate your testimonies, the more you will see the hand of God in your life.

_____

_____

_____

_____

_____

_____

_____

_____

_____

_____

"To the law and to the testimony! If they do not speak according to this word, they have no light of dawn."

Isaiah 8:20 (NIV)

October 3

"Silence is the element in which great things fashion themselves together."

Carlyle

How absolutely true this is! An excellent technique for overcoming tension is to set aside a few minutes each day to observe absolute quietness. Retire to a quiet place. Refuse to talk or do anything, and instead flood your mind with peace by saying the verse below repeatedly and quietly to yourself:

_____
_____
_____
_____
_____
_____
_____

"You will keep in perfect peace him whose mind is steadfast, because he trusts in you."

Isaiah 26:3 (NIV)

October 4

On a flight from Abuja to Lagos, I sat next to a middle-aged, top-flight banker, a man who had distinguished himself in the world of finance. During our inspiring dialogue, he said, "I have been uncommonly blessed with Divine favor. I always had complete confidence that I would eventually succeed and attain my goals. Life is strange. When it realizes that you are not going to submit, no matter what obstacles it places in your path, and that you can't be drained of your enthusiasm and determination, it gives you everything you ask for."

"A lion, mighty among beasts, who retreats before nothing."

Proverbs 30:30 (NIV)

October 5

As a student, I had the rare privilege of listening to Bishop Norman Vincent Peale speak at a small, countryside chapel in Oxfordshire, England. Peale was bishop of the Marble Collegiate Church in New York, and he authored the all-time classic, The Power of Positive Thinking. I remain fascinated, to this day by his characterization of divine grace. Hear him: "God's grace, the condition of being in His favor, is like sunshine. It indiscriminately showers light on all. Those who stand under the sun immerse themselves in the warmth of its rays and receive full benefit from them. Those who hide under the tree deprive themselves of the sun."

_____

_____

_____

_____

_____

_____

_____

_____

"See to it that no-one misses the grace of God."

Hebrews 12:15 (NIV)

October 6

Some people collect stamps as a hobby. Some collect old coins, while still others collect old maps. My own hobby is a bit unusual. I collect people! My wife can testify to this. I make friends anywhere. At the airport. In the bank. Anywhere and everywhere. It brings me out of myself and allows me to reach out to others. I learned it from Bishop Norman V. Peale. He said, "It's because human relationships touch life in its deepest meaning that we are taught to love people, and in so doing, we get very close to satisfying life's deepest desires." Notice the warm glow in your heart when you take an interest in another person.

_____
_____
_____
_____
_____
_____
_____
_____

"Whoever finds his life will lose it, and whoever loses his life for my sake will find it."

Matthew 10:39 (NIV)

October 7

A tailor once told me that clothes look better and last longer if their pockets are emptied of all items like cash, pens, and cards, at night. We can extend the process to mind emptying. Before retiring to bed, empty your mind of all irritations, regrets, resentments, and anxieties into an imaginary wastebasket. This way, you go to sleep relieved of energy-sapping thoughts and wake up refreshed with energy and vitality.

_____
_____
_____
_____
_____
_____
_____
_____
_____
_____

"Do not conform any longer to the pattern of this world, but be transformed by the renewing of your mind."

Romans 12:2 (NIV)

October 8

Those who are certain of the outcome can afford to wait, and without anxiety. When things do not happen as you had planned, remind yourself to be infinitely patient. You must learn to fine tune your understanding of God's timing. He gives according to His own schedule, regardless of your demands, for not even a single leaf will dare to fall from the tree unless God wills it. When you have understood the subtle art of communion with the silent voice of the universal will, and the time is right, what you desire will come to you effortlessly.

"It is not for you to know the times or dates the Father has set by his own authority."

Acts 1:7 (NIV)

October 9

One habit you must inculcate is this: learn from successful failures! Believe it or not, successful people fail far more often than unsuccessful people, for after all, failure is really no more than an opportunity to more intelligently begin all over again.

_____
_____
_____
_____
_____
_____
_____
_____
_____
_____
_____
_____
_____

"The way of a fool seems right to him, but a wise man listens to advice."

Proverbs 12:15 (NIV)

October 10

Kevin glanced downwards at Kunle's shoes.

Kevin: *"Kunle, the soles and heels of your shoes are completely worn out. These shoes are expired!"*

Kunle: *"Well, at least, that means I'm back on my feet, while waiting for the new shoes that will surely come to replace these ones!"*

Such expectant hope! Such incurable optimism! That should always be your attitude towards material inadequacy.

"Be joyful in hope, patient in affliction, faithful in prayer."

Romans 12:12 (NIV)

October 11

Over the years, I have observed something. Most of the people who sit on the front row at church, in lectures, and at workshops are those who come with great expectations. They usually come prepared to learn, and so they take good notes and listen with rapt attention. These wise people are the real winners, because they plan to win, prepare to win, and expect to win.

_____

_____

_____

_____

_____

_____

_____

_____

_____

_____

"Let the wise listen and add to their learning, and let the discerning get guidance."

Proverbs 1:5 (NIV)

October 12

Pastor: *"Brother Sam, if you had two houses, would you be willing to give up one to support God's work?"*

Brother Sam: *"Of course! I'd love to. I only wish I had two houses."*

Pastor: *"If you had a million naira, could you give half a million to God?"*

Brother Sam: *"Certainly! I only wish I had that kind of money!"*

Pastor: *"If you had two cars, would you give up one in furtherance of God's work?"*

Brother Sam shifted uneasily from one foot to the other, and spluttered: "Now, that's not fair! You know I have two cars!" So, can you see how easy it is for us to proclaim our generosity when we have only little?

Refuse to give grudgingly. Give purposefully. Give selflessly. Give gladly.

_____

_____

_____

"[Give] not reluctantly or under compulsion, for God loves a cheerful giver."

2 Corinthians 9:7 (NIV)

October 13

As a medical student, I once had to lend my pathology notebook to a colleague who had accumulated a back log of lecture notes during one of his "unavoidable" absences. A month later, during a teaching ward round, I asked him to loan me his stethoscope to examine a patient with. He flatly refused. I was stunned! That was many years ago. I have since learned that going out of one's way to be nice to someone shouldn't necessarily be with the expectation of even a word of appreciation. We must learn to love even those who won't reciprocate.

———————————————————————
———————————————————————
———————————————————————
———————————————————————
———————————————————————
———————————————————————
———————————————————————
———————————————————————

"Love your enemies, bless them that curse you, do good to them that hate you, and pray for them which despitefully use you, and persecute you."

Matthew 5:44 (KJV)

October 14

"Without a rich heart, wealth is an ugly beggar."

Ralph Waldo Emerson

One of the most important spiritual laws of creating affluence is tithing. Tithing means paying to God a certain portion of your income without conditions attached. When you tithe, a vacuum is created that attracts even more of what you have given.

_____

_____

_____

_____

_____

_____

_____

_____

_____

_____

"Will a man rob God? Yet you rob me. But you ask, How do we rob you? In tithes and offerings."

Malachi 3:8 (NIV)

October 15

A fellowship of excellence exists among the wise. Partake of it. For free or for a fee. Every student is someone's teacher, and every teacher someone's student. For instance, did you know that Socrates taught Plato? And that Plato taught Aristotle? And that Aristotle taught Alexander the Great?

From whom will you learn?

_____
_____
_____
_____
_____
_____
_____
_____
_____

"Can a blind man lead a blind man? Will they not both fall into a pit? A student is not above his teacher, but everyone who is fully trained will be like his teacher."

Luke 6:39–40 (NIV)

October 16

Once, I was invited out to dinner at a smart restaurant in the seaside town of Brighton in England. To my utter amazement, my host, a ranking member of the British aristocracy, gave the waiter a tip even before he served us our meal. That evening, I learned that the habit of expressing our gratitude upfront is one of the most invaluable we can ever develop. Needless to say, we got first-class service at that restaurant that fine, summer evening.

From today, start giving thanks for what you have not yet seen. This is a very powerful form of faith.

_____

_____

_____

_____

_____

_____

_____

"But in everything, by prayer and petition, with thanksgiving, present your request to God."

Philippians 4:6 (NIV)

October 17

We have all experienced life's sudden upheavals in the form of unpredictable and unanticipated events. A strong, healthy man drops dead. A loved one is afflicted with a terminal ailment. A wealthy man suddenly goes bankrupt. The lesson in all these is that contrary to his opinion, a man is not the master of his destiny. Our strength, our wisdom, and our skills are nothing compared to dependence on Him who alone knows the end from the beginning.

_____

_____

_____

_____

_____

_____

_____

_____

"The race is not to the swift, or the battle to the strong, nor does food come to the wise or wealth to the brilliant, or favor to the learned, but time and chance happen to them all."

Ecclesiastes 9:11 (NIV)

October 18

Be realistic. If you leave your wallet exposed, you have to be willing and prepared to lose it. A saint strolls down the street with a wallet. The thief sees no saint, but a wallet. For the thief, to whom the wallet belongs is of no consequence. He merely desires to survive. The reality is that thieves exist. They don't just take your wallet. They also rob you of your faith and belief in the innate good of mankind. Take heed.

"Therefore be as shrewd as snakes and as innocent as doves."

Matthew 10:16(NIV)

October 19

A country's president once visited an eminent scientist in his famous laboratory. Presently, they came to a cauldron of boiling, concentrated sulfuric acid.

Scientist: "Your Excellency, do you have faith in science?"

President: "Certainly, professor, certainly!"

The scientist then washed the president's hand in a special solution, and then asked him to use the hand to scoop out some of the acid. Without as much as a blink, the president plunged his hand into the acid, scooping some into his palm—and he was not injured!

_____

_____

_____

_____

_____

_____

_____

"We accept man's testimony, but God's testimony is greater."

1 John 5:9 (NIV)

October 20

Refuse to brood over the past.

Refuse to be fearful about the future.

Rather, remain supremely concentrated in the present, and the right response will come to you to meet every situation as it occurs.

_____
_____
_____
_____
_____
_____
_____
_____
_____
_____
_____

"Forget the former things. Do not dwell on the past."

Isaiah 43:18 (NIV)

October 21

Celebrate the successes of others as you would have them celebrate yours.

A great sign of mental health is to be glad when others achieve and to rejoice with them. Refuse to compare yourself or your achievements with others, but make your comparisons only with yourself. Maintain a constant competition with yourself and yourself alone. This will compel you to attain higher standards and achievements. Refuse to defeat yourself by holding jealous or spiteful thoughts. Think straight, with love, hope, and optimism, and you will attain your own unique brand of success.

"Rejoice with them that do rejoice, and weep with them that weep."

Romans 12:15 (KJV)

October 22

Perhaps the most amazingly simple fact of our existence that I have discovered in my personal travails is this: this moment shall pass. Indeed, whatever the sorrow, failure, or disappointment, it shall pass. Whatever the joy, elation, or euphoria, it shall pass. The past is gone forever, and it's only your thoughts and actions in the present moment that matter as a prelude to making better choices for the future.

_____
_____
_____
_____
_____
_____
_____
_____
_____
_____

"Now is your time of grief but I will see you again, and you will rejoice, and no-one will take away your joy."

John 16:22 (NIV)

October 23

Take a break. Restore your body and your soul. It doesn't have to be a two-week vacation. Mentally re-create a peaceful scene. Sit quietly and pray. The world can wait. Believe it or not, the world will go on without you. Refuse to take important decisions when you are tired, because that dark state of the mind will impair your judgment. Escape from the world for a few minutes. Even God took a break.

"And He rested on the seventh day from all his work which He had made."

Genesis 2:2 (KJV)

October 24

It is foolhardy to reject criticism, for in order to improve, you need to know what needs improving. So, resolve today to become comfortable with criticism. Realize that it is practically impossible to please everyone all the time. Realize also that in attaining success in any form, you will inevitably elicit criticism from those who are jealous and angry because you left them behind. On a lighter note, is it not also true that you are a candidate for criticism because you have the good fortune to be alive? After all, did you ever see anyone kick a dead dog?

_____

_____

_____

_____

_____

_____

_____

_____

"He who ignores discipline despises himself, but whoever heeds correction gains understanding."

Proverbs 15:32 (NIV)

October 25

"The best helping hand you will ever find is at the end of your own arm."

John Mason

So, your aunt won't help you out financially. Your well connected uncle won't give you an introductory note to his minister friend. Refuse to despise or resent them. Forgive them. Make excuses for them, such as they have enough challenges of their own. Then promptly take responsibility for your own life and your own success by asking God to show you His way.

"I will instruct you and teach you in the way you should go, I will counsel you and watch over you."

Psalm 32:8 (NIV)

October 26

God's purposeful wisdom in according some people more material blessings than others is, quite simply, not disputable. He not only supplies all our needs, He gives us extra so we can meet the needs of others.

_____

_____

_____

_____

_____

_____

_____

_____

_____

_____

_____

"And God is able to make all grace abound to you, so that in all things at all times, having all that you need, you will abound in every good work."

2 Corinthians 9:8 (NIV)

October 27

"Great projects are always built from a blueprint. Consider yourself a great project. So who is your blueprint?"

Jim Rohn

To succeed, you must model success. All around you are people who have achieved the kind of success you desire. They are potential models or mentors. Decide today to adopt their strategies. If you can't have much personal contact with them, read their books, listen to their tapes, and attend their speaking engagements. Appreciate them through thank-you notes, text messages or support for their work.

"Therefore I urge you to imitate me."

1 Corinthians 4:16 (NIV)

October 28

Know one thing for sure: winners do not quit; and quitters do not win.

"Fight the good fight of the faith."

1 Timothy 6:12 (NIV)

October 29

I have always reserved a very healthy respect for the feminine brand of humor. I once visited a couple, family friends of mine, at their well-appointed home in Lagos, Nigeria. They had only just been blessed with a new addition to the family. The wife looked extremely tired and frustrated, and was quite obviously dissipated of all energy.

Husband: *"Never forget, dear, the hand that rocks the cradle rules the world"*

Wife: *"Oh, in that case please come and rule the world for a while. I am tired of being queen!"*

_____

_____

_____

_____

_____

"So in everything, do to others what you would have them do to you."

Matthew 7:12 (NIV)

October 30

Vision and focus are two traits that are indispensable to anyone who will be great. Today, pray that you may have the grace to know your calling by vision, and then to abide in that calling by focus.

"Each one should remain in the situation which he was in when God called him. Brothers, each man, as responsible to God, should remain in the situation God called him to."

1 Corinthians 7:20–24 (NIV)

October 31

If you are a man of great knowledge, people will have great respect for you. If you are a man of great wisdom, people will have great reverence for you. And if you are a man of both great knowledge and great wisdom, you will be the most eminent of men.

But in real terms, people don't care how much you know, or how much wisdom you have, unless they know how much you care.

"Let us not love with words or tongue, but with actions and in truth."

1 John 3:18 (NIV)

November 1

No one can truly access his higher self without the practice of meditation, which involves intense concentration on a word, prayer or scripture, to the exclusion of all other thoughts. The mind experiences abstract levels of the thinking process and ultimately transcends to the state of pure awareness. It is during meditation that subconscious activity is at its peak, making it the most fertile ground for planting prayer. During meditation, blood pressure comes down, stress is alleviated, while insomnia and anxiety are relieved. Also, because of increased brain wave activity, there is increased attention span, creativity, and learning ability. Finally, the effects of meditation last into your daily activity and you become a calmer and more serene person.

Learn to meditate.

"But his delight is in the law of the Lord, and in his law doth he meditate day and night."

Psalm 1:2 (NIV)

November 2

We might choose to view luck from another perspective. It is so easy and so convenient to ascribe good fortune or success to luck, isn't it? But this approach might be too simplistic as, in actual fact, good things don't just happen. They seem to come to those who prepare for them and who are moving in their direction. Put in other words, what we commonly call luck is what results when preparation collides with opportunity.

"Do you see a man skilled in his work? He will serve before kings; he will not serve before obscure men."

Proverbs 22:29 (NIV)

November 3

Mary, a poorly-paid office clerk, arrived only to find a letter under the door to her one-room dwelling. The letter read: "Dear Mary, I shall be visiting at 10:00 a.m. sharp tomorrow, Saturday. Lots of love. Jesus." Mary trembled and thought, "Why would the Lord visit a nobody like me? Worse still, I have no food to offer Him." She hurried out and spent her last N200 on a loaf of bread, a tin of sardines and a tin of milk. On her way back home, a miserable old man, dressed only in rags which did nothing to protect him from the bitter, cold harmattan, accosted her. "Lady, I have not eaten for three days. Please help me." With great reluctance and superhuman effort, she gave him the food meant for the Lord, wondering how she would replace it. She then took off her cardigan and gave it to the old man. A shivering Mary arrived her doorway only to find another letter, which read; "It was nice seeing you again. Thank you for the bread, sardines and milk. Thank you also for the sweater. Bless your kind heart. Lots of love. Jesus."

_____

_____

_____

"Is it not to share your food with the hungry and to provide the poor wanderer with shelter, when you see the naked to clothe him?"

Isaiah 58:7 (NIV)

November 4

One of the greatest and most potent secrets of success in life is to find a human need and fill it.

The popular Nigerian musician, Sunny Nneji, composed and sang the beautiful, melodious song titled oruka. This song has emerged a swan song, call it an anthem of sorts, at virtually all wedding receptions in Nigeria. It nostalgically epitomizes the wedding ring as the symbol of holy matrimony. He had, wittingly or unwittingly assuaged a yearning for a nuptial celebratory song. The song has become an all-time chart topper.

What human need can you skillfully fill?

_____

_____

_____

_____

_____

"If the axe is dull and its edge unsharpened, more strength is needed, but skill will bring success."

Ecclesiastes 10:10 (NIV)

November 5

"The real secret of happiness is to admire without necessarily desiring."

R.H. Bradley

Much of human despondency is caused by innate discontent. The acquisitive nature of man is one of his basest instincts. But this instinct can become inappropriately exaggerated if not kept in check. The reason is that your little self, that non-spiritual aspect of you, can never be quite satisfied. As soon as you satisfy its yearning for a beautiful home, it cries out for an even bigger home. Or car. Or more clothes. Yes, the material, good things of life form part of God's blessings, but we must always ask for the grace to develop sufficient spirituality to curb an inordinate need for material gratification. We must avoid greed.

"I know what it is to be in need, and I know what it is to have plenty. I have learned the secret of being content in any and every situation, whether well fed or hungry, whether living in plenty or in want."

Philippians 4:12 (NIV)

November 6

The hilariously amusing story is told of a German who is in the strange habit of bursting into very loud laughter in the woods near his home in Berlin. He was taken to court by a group of early morning joggers who claimed that his peals of laughter distracted them on their runs. The judge ordered him to stop his laughing escapades or face the prospect of a six-month jail term. But this was not before the man had entered a defense, "I go there to laugh for twenty minutes every day to relieve stress. For me, it had become a health routine, like regular exercise."

_____

_____

_____

_____

_____

_____

_____

_____

_____

"A cheerful heart is good medicine, but a crushed spirit dries up the bones."

Proverbs 17:22 (NIV)

November 7

King Herod, resplendent in his royal robes, had delivered an oratory to an audience, and in a bid to curry his favor, they eulogized him, saying, "This is the voice of a God, not of man." Herod lapped up the praise, refusing to acknowledge God as the true and only recipient of such praise. Instantly, an angel struck him and he died a painful death. In contradistinction, Paul miraculously healed a cripple and witnesses shouted in reference to Paul and Barnabas, "The Gods have come down to us in the likeness of men." They were both aghast, insisting that they were but only mere mortals.

"Not to us, O Lord, not to us, but to your name be the glory, because of your love and faithfulness."

Psalm 115:1 (NIV)

November 8

"Man is only truly great when he acts from passion."

Benjamin Disraeli

Three men were part of the construction team at the site of a new cathedral that was still at foundation level. A passerby curiously asked them the same question:

Passerby:	*"What are you doing?"*
First Mason:	*"I'm molding blocks."*
Passerby:	*"My brother, what are you doing?"*
Second Mason:	*"I'm molding blocks that will be used for the foundation of a building."*
Passerby:	*"What are you doing?"*
Third Mason:	*"I am building a cathedral."*

Who of these three men is the one with passion, vision, and purpose?

"Where there is no vision, the people perish."

Proverbs 29:18 (KJV)

November 9

One evening, I was getting prepared to attend a dinner event. I wanted to put on an already worn white shirt and was inspecting it carefully to see if it were still clean. My wife, noticing, called out to me, "Remember, dear, if it's doubtful, don't." I promptly settled for another shirt.

The principle of "If doubtful, don't" can and should be applied to questionable matters of conscience. When faced with questionable practices and a troubled conscience, make this principle your guideline.

_____

_____

_____

_____

_____

_____

"But the man who has doubts is condemned if he eats, because his eating is not from faith, and everything that does not come from faith is sin."

Romans 14:23 (NIV)

November 10

People commonly say things like, "I'm only a gardener," or "I'm only a driver," or "I'm only an average student." God chose Gideon to conquer the Midianites, calling him "a mighty man of valor." Gideon, however, thought otherwise, claiming that his clan was the weakest in the land and that he was the least in his family. But God insisted, giving Gideon only three hundred men to help him achieve victory.

Refuse to denigrate yourself. Refuse to underestimate your usefulness. There is no such person as a nobody in God's eyes.

"But God chose the foolish things of the world to shame the wise; God chose the weak things of the world to shame the strong."

1 Corinthians 1:27 (NIV)

November 11

An extremely wealthy acquaintance of mine has a seven-year-old daughter who is constantly waited upon by servants. One night, she was afraid to climb a dark staircase all by herself. Her father told her to conquer her fear by asking Jesus to go up the stairs with her. When she reached the top she said loudly, "Thank you, Jesus. You may go now."

Most of us are very much like her. We tend to treat God like a vending machine. We see God mainly as a problem solver. When His merciful solutions come, we thank Him courteously and then forget about Him until the next crisis.

_____

_____

_____

_____

_____

_____

"But they soon forgot what he had done and did not wait for his counsel."

Psalm 106:13 (NIV)

November 12

A man stood on the river bank holding a small box filled with gold coins. With tears streaming down his face, he would, one after the other, pick a coin and toss it into the river. A passerby observed him for a while, and then went close to him.

Passerby: "Why are you throwing away the coins one after the other?"

The man: "To learn non-attachment to riches."

Passerby: "In that case, why don't you simply throw the whole box into the river at once?"

The man: (gasping in anguish) "Oh no! I couldn't possibly do that. It would be too painful to bear."

_____

_____

_____

_____

"Indeed, it is easier for a camel to pass through the eye of a needle than for a rich man to enter the kingdom of God."

Luke 18:25 (NIV)

November 13

A crafty cat had killed virtually all the rats in an uncompleted building. The rats therefore went into conference to decide on a course of action. An old, black rat was thought to be very wise indeed. He said, "Let us hang a bell to the cat's neck. When we hear it ring, we shall know she's coming and can get out of her way."

"Excellent. Splendid." They said in excited unison, while one rat ran to get the bell.

"So, who amongst us will hang the bell on the cat's neck?"

"Not me," "Not me," they said, one after the other. And they all scampered to safety.

This is the origin of the common saying, "Who will bell the cat?"

_____

_____

_____

"Here I am, send me!"

Isaiah 6:8 (NIV)

November 14

Knowledge, it is rightly said, is power, and the basic unit of the acquisition of knowledge is information. Therefore, you must deliberately seek information to become knowledgeable. To exploit the power that is inherent in knowledge acquisition, henceforth, anytime you learn new information, ask yourself three questions:

- *Where can I use it?*
- *When can I use it?*
- *Who else needs to know it?*

_____

_____

_____

_____

_____

_____

_____

_____

"Teach me good judgement and knowledge."

Psalm 119:66 (NIV)

November 15

We are all businessmen, in one form or the other. Since God created us in His own image, it follows from spiritual logic that God is the ultimate businessman. The scriptures state clearly that God will give more to those who already have. This is because He knows that those who have more have demonstrated mastery over what they have been given. God will not "do business" with those who show no signs of potential return on investment. He will only invest in you if you demonstrate an ability to handle properly what He has given you. Put quite simply, God is looking for fruitfulness. When He finds it, He will reward it with even more fruit.

_____

_____

_____

_____

_____

_____

_____

"To everyone who has, more will be given, but as for the one who has nothing, even what he has will be taken away."

Luke 19:26 (NIV)

November 16

As a medical student, I was necessarily exposed to a seemingly endless mass of both simple and complicated medical jargon and information. Even then, my clinical teachers always taught a basic fact: common things occur commonly. In other words, a simple view of and a simple attitude toward human ailment is often the best approach.

The corollary of this is seen in prayer. Most of us labor under the illusion that prayer is effective only when it is long, convoluted, and complicated. Prayer can be quite simple, yet powerful. Today, say this very simple and innocent prayer:

"Dear God, give me the ability to face life with wisdom and patience."

_____

_____

_____

_____

"And when you pray, do not keep on babbling like pagans for they think they will be heard because of their many words."

Matthew 6:7 (NIV)

November 17

Today, I urge you to consciously experience and express a feeling of appreciation for anything or anyone that you consider of value in your life, especially your loved ones, and even those material things with which God has blessed you. The truth is that all too often, we take what we have for granted and may even treat it with contempt. It's not until we lose it that we finally appreciate its real value in our lives.

_____

_____

_____

_____

_____

_____

_____

_____

_____

_____

_____

_____

"Give thanks in all circumstances."

1 Thessalonians 5:18 (NIV)

November 18

Actually, what ultimately becomes of you is a reflection of what your deep, driving desire is. As your desire is, so is your will. As your will is, so is your deed. As your deed is, so is your destiny. However, you should always have it at the back of your mind that you may propose, but God will dispose.

"Many are the plans in a man's heart, but it is the Lord's purpose that prevails."

Proverbs 19:21 (NIV)

November 19

"One's philosophy is not best expressed in words. It is expressed in the choices one makes. In the long run, we shape our lives and we shape ourselves. The process never ends until we die. And, the choices we make are ultimately our own responsibility."

Eleanor Roosevelt

This assertion is very insightful because the greatest gift that God gave us is the gift of life. The second greatest is the power of choice.

_____

_____

_____

_____

_____

_____

_____

_____

_____

"Give therefore thy servant an understanding heart to judge thy people, that I may discern between good and bad."

1 Kings 3:9 (NIV)

November 20

The usual thing is to be invited out to dinner by people superior to us, isn't it? Such people would usually be role models for us, and they are likely to be older, and much more successful than us. We aspire to achieve their brand of success, and we tend to model ourselves after them.

Do something revolutionary. Turn convention on its head by saving up some hard-earned money and inviting such a person out to dinner. You will be amazed at the amount of wisdom that will be availed you that evening.

_____

_____

_____

_____

_____

_____

_____

"I tell you the truth, no servant is greater than his master, nor is a messenger, greater than the one who sent him."

John 13:16 (NIV)

November 21

It would seem that prayer and work are two wheels of a cart. Prayer releases God's favor, while work unleashes the force of man. When God's favor collides with your force, the extraordinary in you manifests. You must work at everything for which you pray. To see the fruit, you must till the garden.

"For by strength shall no man prevail."

1 Samuel 2:9 (KJV)

331

November 22

Faith is an unshakeable conviction that has the sole goal of reaching what it hopes for using the vehicle of a plan. My greatest personal discovery is that when I pray for a goal, God answers with a plan. Yes, God does give us miracles, but it would seem that because of our inordinate fixation on them, we fail to recognize that He mostly answers our prayers with a plan.

_____
_____
_____
_____
_____
_____
_____
_____
_____
_____
_____

"For I know the plans I have for you, declares the Lord, plans to prosper you and not to harm you, plans to give you hope and a future."

Jeremiah 29:11 (NIV)

November 23

At my alma mater, St. Paul's College, Zaria, in Nigeria's North-Western flank, those who decidedly did not take part in approved games were branded passengers. Life, however, is no simple game. It is a rough and tumble experience. For you to win in it, you must be in the driver's seat. You must respond to life's ups and downs rather than react to them. Be proactive.

_____
_____
_____
_____
_____
_____
_____
_____
_____
_____

"Be very careful, then, how you live - not as unwise, but as wise, making the most of every opportunity."

Ephesians 5:15–16 (NIV)

November 24

In life, to win you must first lose. This sounds paradoxical, doesn't it? Yes, you must first lose your pointless fears and unwholesome habits. These are the "junk of life." You have enough trials and tribulations to contend with, why endure those things that you should discard. You will recall how Bartimeus, the blind man, threw aside his coat as Jesus approached. Ask for the grace to know what to keep in your life and what to eliminate.

"Let us throw off everything that hinders."

Hebrews 12:1 (NIV)

November 25

All advances, whether spiritual, emotional or material, are invariably preceded by a fall of some kind. Such falls may indeed be so devastating that we feel completely traumatized. However, we should view those falls with gratitude rather than dismay. This is because of the lessons contained in them.

"It was good for me to be afflicted so that I might learn your decrees."

Psalm 119:71 (NIV)

November 26

I have never ceased to be amazed at the propensity of my countrymen to grab titles, which end up becoming unseemly appendages to their names. This fetish for titles, and by extension societal recognition, can, to any discerning mind, only be a symptom of an incurable need to gratify and glorify the ego. Yet, glory, in all things, belongs only to God. Worry less about titles and recognition, and let your accomplishments speak for themselves.

_____

_____

_____

_____

_____

_____

_____

_____

_____

_____

"We were not looking for praise from men, not from you or anyone else."

1 Thessalonians 2:6 (NIV)

November 27

Our time in this lifetime is very short, and because of this, the time at our disposal becomes quite precious—every second, minute, and hour. Every moment that you live is an irreplaceable resource and a limited supply. While we strive towards eternal life, we must remember that no matter how important, beautiful, powerful, or wealthy we may be, time waits for no one. The fragile beauty of our existence is aptly captured below.

"As for man, his days are like grass, he flourishes like a flower of the field; the wind blows over it and it is gone, and its place remembers it no more."

Psalm 103:15–16 (NIV)

November 28

As a student in England, I enjoyed playing music as loud as my speakers would permit. I would subject my hostel mates to unspeakably loud pop music at hours as unholy as 2:00 a.m. Although I'd apologize when they complained, deep inside I was rebelliously remorseless. With the wisdom of hindsight, I now know I ought to have been considerate enough to engage in healthy compromise. It was unfair to keep them awake at such hours. Healthy compromise is all about creating win-win possibilities, and this means seeing things through the eyes of others in any situation.

_____
_____
_____
_____
_____
_____
_____
_____

"Hold them in the highest regard in love because of their work. Live in peace with each other."

1 Thessalonians 5:13 (NIV)

November 29

"A common past is good. It unites your yesterdays. But common goals are better. They unite your tomorrows."

Bishop T.D. Jakes

Cultivate relationships that will allow you to embrace the future, while moving beyond the "good old days." Refuse to linger for too long on the memory lane. The time has come to stop rehearsing the beginning and to settle down to write the rest of your story. Forge ahead!

"Forgetting those things which are behind, and reaching forth unto those things which are before."

Philippians 3:13 (KJV)

November 30

For most people, their collection of past mistakes and blunders are a prison of sorts. Guilt and regrets are the prison wardens, holding them captive for years on end. Tragically however, most of such people fail to realize that the key to freedom is in their hands. They refuse to use the key, prolonging their prison sentence. Today, unlock those prison gates and release yourself from the burden of past mistakes. Remember, today is the first day of the rest of your life.

"Let the wicked forsake his way and the evil man his evil thoughts, let him turn to the Lord."

Isaiah 55:7 (NIV)

December 1

Today is the first day of the last month of the year. How have you fared throughout the year? It is time to do the year's assessment of each area of your life—family, finances, career progress, spiritual growth, etc. Realize that to get more in the coming year, you must become more. So, as you prepare to end this year and commence another, identify what needs to be modified and what needs to be eliminated. You must continue to improve in each area of your life. This is called re-engineering. Better still, call it re-branding yourself.

_____

_____

_____

_____

_____

_____

_____

_____

_____

_____

"The old has gone, the new has come."

2 Corinthians 5:17 (NIV)

December 2

"Spirituality can be defined as the active maintenance and sustenance of a connectivity with the Lord. It is this spirituality that will allow you to develop a do-it-yourself commitment to seeking God's voice. Today, I decree that your spiritual ears may be opened to the voice of God."

Bishop David O. Oyedepo

"This is what we speak, not in words taught us by human wisdom but in words taught by the spirit, expressing spiritual truths in spiritual words. The man without the spirit does not accept the things that come from the spirit of God, for they are foolishness to him."

1 Corinthians 2:13–14 (NIV)

December 3

In practical terms, prosperity is probably in two forms. There is sur-vival prosperity, and there is Abrahamic abundance. The way to proceed from the first to the second is simply to become a channel of blessing for others. We achieve this by doing three things:

- *Giving to the kingdom of God.*
- *Giving to the poor within His kingdom.*
- *Giving to the poor outside His kingdom.*

"Command them to do good, to be rich in good deeds, and to be generous and willing to share."

1 Timothy 6:18 (NIV)

December 4

God has an agenda for the poor. You are part of that agenda. He is very mindful of the poor, and so you must refuse to despise the poor. To take care of them is to gain God's blessings. Add the poor to your budget.

_____
_____
_____
_____
_____
_____
_____
_____
_____
_____
_____
_____

"He who is kind to the poor lends to the Lord and He will reward him for what he has done."

Proverbs 19:17 (NIV)

December 5

Let us look at generosity from another perspective. Your desire to give unconditionally ought to be a confident acknowledgment that your possessions have come from an infinite, inexhaustible supply. It follows therefore that you should never experience a scarcity consciousness because you know that you are connected to that infinite supply simply by being a part of the unbroken cycle of giving and receiving.

"Now He who supplies seed to the sower and bread for food will also supply and increase your store of seed and will enlarge the harvest of your righteousness. You will be made rich in every way so that you can be generous on every occasion."

2 Corinthians 9:10–11 (NIV)

December 6

All cultures subscribe to the maxim, "That person is wise who knows what to say and when to say it." Indeed, he who guards his tongue well preaches a great sermon. An ancient Persian sage said: "A lengthy tongue, an early death."

The Greeks would say, "The tongue is boneless, and so small and weak, yet it can crush and kill."

And yet the Hebrews declared, "Though your feet may slip, don't let your tongue."

Finally, the Bible says, "Who keeps his tongue keeps his soul."

_____

_____

_____

_____

"The tongue is also a fire, a world of evil among the parts of the body. It corrupts the whole person, sets the whole course of his life on fire, and is itself set on fire by hell."

James 3:6 (NIV)

December 7

Beware of what most people think. Most people think like most people do, and this means that most people tend to repeat what others have done or said. Their ideas, not being theirs, tend to be stale concepts held by the vast majority. This is why originality is one of the greatest gifts you can offer yourself.

_____
_____
_____
_____
_____
_____
_____
_____
_____
_____

"And no one puts new wine into old wineskins, or else the new wine will burst the wineskins and be spilled ... But new wine must be put into new wineskins, and both are preserved."

Proverbs 5:37–38 (NIV)

December 8

Winners are always eager to learn and to improve, in the process discovering the secret principles that make things work. They cultivate mentors who can teach them even more. Taking nothing for granted, they are not afraid to discard an idea, admit they were wrong and start all over. To winners, problems are not obstacles. They are merely opportunities they use to stimulate their passion, creativity, and perseverance. Never giving up, they try to discern the secret truths and the celestial laws that make all things a part of the divine order.

"Do not let this book of the law depart from your mouth; meditate on it day and night, so that you may be careful to do everything written in it. Then you will be prosperous and successful."

Joshua 1:8 (NIV)

December 9

An infant lion lost his parents and was raised by a flock of goats, so he grew up thinking he was a goat, too. Although he had the wrong type of teeth, he ate a goat's diet. Of course, he tried to bleat like a goat, instead producing an awkward roar. One day, he met another lion, and not recognizing his kinsman, became as frightened as the real goats. He had lost his true nature, just as happens with most people. Most of us are lions acting like goats our whole life, and those who insist they are lions are called fools and dreamers.

Get rid of the goat so that the lion inside you can wake up!

"A lion, mighty among beasts, who retreats before nothing."

Proverbs 30:30 (NIV)

December 10

A man had been confined to a wheelchair for years, seemingly para-
lyzed from the waist down. One day at the beach, he watched help-
lessly as his son struggled frantically with an ocean wave. Terrified
that the boy would drown and with no assistance in sight, he sprang
from the wheelchair to go and save his son. He brought him safely
back to shore and never returned to that wheelchair.

_____
_____
_____
_____
_____
_____
_____
_____
_____
_____
_____

"What is impossible with men is possible with God."

Luke 18:27 (NIV)

December 11

You may not always be able to choose your circumstances, but you can choose your attitude toward them. A friend told me the touching tale of an uncle who was wrongfully convicted for murder and spent ten years awaiting trial, another fifteen years for final judgment to be delivered, and yet another ten years on death row (condemned prisoners cells). In all his travails, he managed to retain his sanity. Finally, on the day he was to be hanged, fresh evidence indicating his innocence prompted the governor to order his immediate release. At the prison gates, he said, "All a man has can be taken from him except the last of the human freedoms—the power to choose one's attitude in all circumstances."

_____

_____

_____

_____

_____

_____

_____

"I can do everything through him who gives m

December 12

Without doubt, our physical appearance is of paramount importance to us. A certain degree of vanity is to be considered quite normal, and each one of us has something with which he or she is not quite satisfied. However, an absolute fixation on perceived imperfections, leading to dysfunction, must give cause for concern.

Remember, always: "You were fearfully and wonderfully made."

_____

_____

_____

_____

_____

_____

_____

_____

_____

_____

"Man looks at the outward appearance, but the Lord looks at the heart."

1 Samuel 16:7 (NIV)

December 13

"When you read, tap from the principles used in the book you have read. To fly on eagle's wings, you must tap on the principles of the eagle. You will have to get on his back and spread out the way he spreads his wings, so as to fly the way he flies. That is why you need to follow the principles of the writer of any book you have read so as to get the results the writer has gotten."

Bishop David O. Oyedepo

This servant of God has said it all. It is for this reason that one can quite safely declare that readers are leaders and leaders are readers.

_____

_____

_____

_____

_____

_____

_____

"Wisdom is supreme, therefore get wisdom. Though it cost all you have, get understanding."

Proverbs 4:7 (NIV)

December 14

One major obstacle to an attitude of gratitude is the habit of complaining. While engaged in active medical practice, I was exposed to a lot of patients who, quite frankly, had nothing wrong with them. They would complain of all sorts of symptoms, but examination and tests would reveal nothing. Refreshingly, however, I attended to a sweet, very old lady one day. Our encounter was a departure from normal.

Doctor: *"Good day, ma'am, how are you today?"*

Patient: *"Oh, I thank God for His little mercies. I have only two teeth left, but lucky me, they are useful because they are opposite each other."*

Learn to count your blessings.

_____

_____

_____

_____

"Do everything without complaining or arguing."

Philippians 2:14 (NIV)

December 15

It took the innocent, but insightful intervention of his six-year-old daughter to cure my friend of his chronic grumbling habit. This was what happened. One day, in the sitting room, the little girl quipped to her mother, "I know what each of us likes. Mary likes ice cream, John likes biscuits, Favour likes chocolates, and Mummy, you like salad."

Alarmed at his exclusion from the list, my friend asked his daughter, "Hey, what about Daddy? What do I like."

She answered promptly, "You like everything we haven't got!"

"Keep your lives free from the love of money and be content with what you have."

Hebrews 13:5 (NIV)

December 16

Your world is not primarily made of the circumstances that surround you. Actually, the thoughts that you think determine the exact kind of world in which you live. That is, you are not what you think you are; rather, what you think, you are.

Wise men, through the ages, have recognized this.

Marcus Aurelius was emperor of Rome 2,000 years ago. He wrote, "Your life is what your thoughts make it." Ralph Waldo Emerson was considered the wisest man in America. He wrote, "A man is what he thinks all day long." And the Bible declares, "As a man thinketh in his heart, so is he."

Change your thoughts, and you change your world.

"For as a man thinketh in his heart, so is he."

Proverbs 23:7 (KJV)

December 17

There are four attributes that one must develop to become and remain a winner. These are: determination, diligence, discipline, and the right attitude. Daniel of the popular biblical story, Daniel in the lion's den, provides us an eloquent example in his possession of this quartet of traits in his commitment to his mission.

_____

_____

_____

_____

_____

_____

_____

_____

_____

_____

"But Daniel resolved not to defile himself with the royal food and wine, and he asked the chief official for permission not to defile himself in this way."

Daniel 1:8 (NIV)

December 18

"You can get everything in life you want if you will only help other people get what they want."

Zig Ziglar

Helping others to fulfill their desires is a sure way to ensure the fulfillment of yours. This is because the best way to motivate others to help you fulfill your goals is to help them fulfill theirs. After all, the basic virtue of life is to serve your fellow being, and through this service, you will increase your value to them.

_____

_____

_____

_____

_____

_____

_____

_____

"Carry each other's burdens, and in this way you will fulfill the law of Christ."

Galatians 6:2 (NIV)

December 19

Many years ago as a student in England, I served on a church fund-raising committee. I asked the vicar from where all the money would come. He answered simply, "From wherever it is at the moment." I now know he meant that God's abundance is everywhere. That is wealth consciousness. It is the absence of money worries. A truly wealthy person's attention is never focused on money alone. You may have millions in the bank, but if you think all the time about it, worrying about getting more, not having enough, or even losing it, then you are actually poor. The fact is that God's supply is inexhaustible. Refuse to let money take over your life. See it for what it is and no more.

"Command those who are rich in this present world not to be arrogant nor to put their hope in wealth, which is so uncertain, but to put their hope in God."

1 Timothy 6:17 (NIV)

December 20

Two farmers met and got talking. One was from Lagos, Nigeria's commercial nerve center, while the other was from Abuja, Nigeria's capital city.

Abuja farmer: *"How big is your farm?"*

Lagos farmer: *"Very big. I have more than sixty acres."*

Abuja farmer: *(Rather surprised and not willing to be outdone) "See, if I started out in my pickup van at sunrise, by sunset I would still be on my land."*

Lagos farmer: *(Looking amused) "Funny, I once had a pickup like that. The slowest thing I ever knew!"*

Boastful pride. A self-sufficient attitude. We need to avoid these. We need to be humble.

"A man's pride brings him low, but a man of lowly spirit gains honor."

Proverbs 29:23 (NIV)

December 21

I was out driving to attend to a medical emergency one night when an oncoming car cut sharply left in front of me. In self-righteous indignation, I plonked on my horn to announce to the person just how nearly he had caused an accident by his careless driving. A few minutes later, when I'd parked my car, the same car pulled up beside me and the driver got out, saying, "Perhaps you would care to put on your headlights while driving at night." I was the one who had almost caused the accident. In my inordinate haste, I had forgotten to turn on my headlights.

Be quick to judge yourself and slow to judge others.

_____
_____
_____
_____
_____
_____

"Do not judge, and you will not be judged. Do not condemn, and you will not be condemned."

Luke 6:37 (NIV)

December 22

Today, say this special prayer:

"Dear God, show me where I fit into Your plan, lead me in the way I ought to go, and I will forever live in Your will."

"Teach me your way, O Lord, and I will walk in your truth."

Psalm 86:11 (NIV)

December 23

Creative imagination, which is actually faith in practice, is greater than knowledge. This is because knowledge is merely to grasp what is, while imagination, backed by faith, reaches out to what can be. This is why to be a man of vision is to be a man of greatness. Vision is the ultimate result of creative imagination and visualization, conferring on you the ability to go beyond present reality and to create and invent what does not yet exist. From today, start to engage in creative daydreaming. Employ these two scenes:

Scene 1: *See yourself where you want to be.*
Scene 2: *See yourself going through the processes that will take you there.*

_____

_____

_____

_____

_____

"Therefore, I tell you, whatever you ask for in prayer, believe that you have received it, and it will be yours."

Mark 11:24 (NIV)

December 24

A man at a traffic intersection absent-mindedly and blindly followed the car just ahead of him, whose driver had decided to jump the traffic light. The result was a serious, multiple-car accident.

To follow the leader is wise, but to cross-check his teaching is wiser still.

_____

_____

_____

_____

_____

_____

_____

_____

_____

_____

"They received the message with great eagerness and examined the scriptures every day to see if what Paul said was true."

Acts 17:11 (NIV)

December 25

Today, take out time, as you relish your Christmas lunch, to medi-tate on the significance of this day in the life of a Christian. Today is a great day indeed, for it is the birthday of the King of Kings, our Lord and Savior, through whom we have gained eternal life.

_____
_____
_____
_____
_____
_____
_____
_____
_____
_____
_____
_____
_____

"Today in the town of David a savior has been born to you; he is Christ the Lord"

Luke 2:11 (NIV)

December 26

Anger, like dynamite, is a potent explosive. Unless it is handled with wisdom and self-control, it can precipitate devastating damage. If you allow your temper to get the best of you, it will only reveal the worst of you.

"A man's wisdom gives him patience, it is to his glory to overlook an offence."

Proverbs 19:11 (NIV)

December 27

In prayer is contained the most powerful form of spiritual energy available to man. Its power is so rich, so potent, and so mobile that all we need do when we intercede on behalf of someone is to point to the person and God will direct the necessary power to that person. The only condition is to pray according to God's will.

_____

_____

_____

_____

_____

_____

_____

_____

_____

_____

_____

_____

_____

"This is the confidence we have in approaching God, that if we ask anything according to his will, he hears us."

1 John 5:14 (NIV)

December 28

Mothers seem to possess a unique and limitless capacity for showing empathy, gentleness, and compassion. It would also seem that they equally possess a true nobility that allows them to influence the spiritual direction of their children. Clearly, she who gladly fills that role can positively shape her child's destiny.

Today, be thankful for your mother and/or anyone who has been like a mother to you.

Today, be thankful for your mother and/or anyone who has been like a mother to you.

Romans 16:13 (NIV)

December 29

"A great warrior wins the battle even before confronting the enemy."

Sun Tzu
Chinese General

Indeed, life is a battle, not so much against others as against your-self. When you do sufficient battle against yourself and can finally renounce your small self, then your higher self can rise up, giving you the self-discipline and wisdom you need to be touched by celestial grace and to shine like the sun.

"Arise, shine, for your light has come, and the glory of the Lord rises upon you."

Isaiah 60:1 (NIV)

December 30

The supreme secret of success in life is truly a secret. But this is not because anybody is committed to keeping it secret. Rather, it is because only a few people understand it. The secret is contained in a simple sentence:

"The human mind can accomplish whatever it believes in."

When you truly understand these words and allow their import to sink into your consciousness, your success will become yours to claim.

_____
_____
_____
_____
_____
_____
_____

"I tell you the truth, if anyone says to this mountain, go, throw your-self into the sea, and does not doubt in his heart but believes that what he says will happen, it will be done for him."

Mark 11:33 (NIV)

December 31

Today is the last day of the year. What is your verdict on yourself for this year? How have you fared? How would you score yourself as a person of genuine purpose?

Imagine a pilot taking off in a plane without knowing how or where to land it. When your flight through life is over, where and how will you be landing? Here's wishing you a happy and purpose-filled new year ahead, a year that will be filled with love and joy, and which will reveal the very best in you. Shalom.

_____

_____

_____

_____

_____

_____

_____

_____

"I have fought the good fight, I have finished the race, I have kept the faith."

2 Timothy 4:7 (NIV)

42842864R00235

Made in the USA
San Bernardino, CA
11 December 2016